THE EIGHTEENTH-CENTURY PLEASURE GARDENS OF MARYLEBONE
1737–1777

by

MOLLIE SANDS

THE SOCIETY FOR THEATRE RESEARCH
1987

First published 1987
by The Society for Theatre Research
c/o The Theatre Museum
1e Tavistock Street, London WC2E 7PA

ISBN 0 85430 044 9

Printed in Great Britain
at The Bath Press, Avon

Acknowledgements

A visit to the Harvard Collection in 1978 brought to my notice hitherto unknown material concerning Marylebone (or Marybone) Gardens, and decided me to take seriously what had been for years a half-formed project. Special thanks therefore are due to the Curator and staff of that Collection. Subsequently, Richard Bowden, Archivist of the St. Marylebone Local History Collection (City of Westminster Libraries) has inevitably born the brunt of my enquiries. He has encouraged and furthered my research with much patience, and his staff have been very co-operative.

I have had valuable help from the GLC Record Office and History Library, the Guildhall Library, the Portrait Department at the Royal College of Music, the Bodleian Library (John Johnson Collection, Department of Printed Books), the Camden Reference Library at Swiss Cottage, the British Library and the indispensable London Library.

Ron Harris of 'Ye Fireworkes' (The Firework Archive) was generous with his specialist knowledge, and brought the Torre 'Exhibitions' to life for me. Donald Garstang of Colnaghi's traced his firm's connection with Torre; and Gilbert Lawrance, of the St. Marylebone Society, let me have the benefit of his research into Marybone's eighteenth century tavern licences.

Stephen Wildeman, Deputy Keeper of the Prints and

Acknowledgements

Drawings, Fine Art Department of the City of Birmingham Museum and Art Gallery, arranged for me to see the original of 'the Donowell View'.

Hilary Thomas, Susan Moore and Miranda Whyte spent hours at the GLC and the Burney Collection, saving me much time and eyesight. Several colleagues in the Society for Theatre Research gave me useful references and suggestions.

Gratitude is due to Olive Youngs not only for preparing the Index, but for reading the manuscript in a very crude state, and giving me most valuable and constructive criticism, and to Mary Speaight for drawing the sketch map indicating the site of the Gardens in relation to the present line of streets. Anne Merriman typed the manuscript, miraculously producing order out of chaos.

Finally, without the initial encouragement of George Speaight, and his subsequent careful editing, the manuscript would never have reached the printed page, Anyone who enjoys this book must join in my thanks to him.

Contents

Contents

Contents

Contents

Illustrations

ix

All illustrations not otherwise acknowledged are reproduced by permission of the Archives Department, City of Westminster Libraries, Marylebone Library.

Introduction

Madame Tussaud's Waxworks and Planetarium are on the itinerary of every visitor to London, and the literary-minded will cross the Marylebone Road to see the handsome early nineteenth-century church where in 1846 Robert Browning was married to Elizabeth Barrett, who lived nearby in Wimpole Street.

Before the Marylebone Road, or St. Marylebone Church or Wimpole Street were built, and even before young Marie Tussaud sat in a Paris prison modelling newly decapitated heads, Marylebone was a village.[1] Just round the corner from where the church now stands was a rural place of entertainment known as Marybone Gardens between 1737 and 1777. Daniel Defoe wrote between 1724 and 1726:

> Westminster is in a fair way to shake hands with Chelsea, as St. Giles's is with Maribone, ... yet all these put together are still to be called London ... Whither will this monstrous City then extend?[2]

He was voicing an anxiety which filled many minds in the early eighteenth century. A scattering of villages loosely connected to one another and to the twin Cities of London and Westminster still provided oases where people could play at being in the country, but such oases were already threatened. Gardens which had been enjoyed informally became places of formal entertainment, in an effort to preserve their amenities. It is only of recent years that we have called them Pleasure Gardens, to indicate that their purpose was not simply horticulture. At the mid-point of the century there were about sixty such 'Gardens', ranging from the sophisticated Ranelagh, Vauxhall and the less sophisticated Marybone – supplying concerts, fireworks and space to promenade on a fairly large scale – to the smaller Tea Gardens with possibly bowls and skittles.

Half a century of semi-rural life was left to Marylebone before it was swallowed up by Defoe's 'monstrous City' and building crept up to the Outer or Great Park. From 1737 to 1776 Marybone Gardens flourished as a place where people could pay for walking in the fresh air, listening to music and partaking of refreshments.

Their origin went back to the seventeenth century or earlier, and Pepys visited them as he visited 'Fox Hall' which turned into Spring Gardens, Vauxhall, a few years earlier than Daniel Gough 'opened' Marylebone. Vauxhall and Marybone both progressed from the informal to the formal, to suit the needs of the age.

The lay-out of the seventeenth-century gardens which Pepys knew was typical of the period, formal and contained: a bowling green was in the centre, quickset hedges were cut with topiary art to represent town walls, there were circular gravel walks and an outer brick wall enclosed the property, according to the Sainthill plan[3]:

> Then we abroad to Marrowbone, and there walked in the Gardens . . . and a pretty place it is (1668).

Bowls and skittles were popular in the seventeenth and early eighteenth century and there were several Greens or Alleys in the village. Marksmanship was also practised in the grounds of the Rose in 1691; gentlemen were invited to enter for a competition to be held there and to view the plate offered for a prize at a Gunsmith's in Catherine Street,

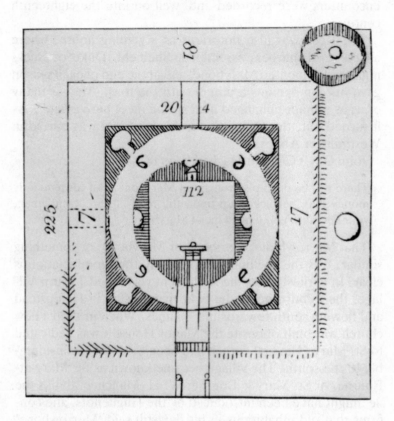

The Samuel Sainthill map, 1659

Strand. Less pleasant was the sport of dog fighting, mentioned by John Gay. Indeed the manners and pastimes of the early eighteenth century had little of the polish and elegance we associate with the period.

The open fields of Marylebone and its Park were very suitable for duelling. Sir Charles Blunt and the Earl of Essex fought in the neighbourhood in Queen Elizabeth's day, and encounters were recorded until well on into the eighteenth century.

The Rose was also notorious as a gaming house, where all the card-sharpers assembled. Sheffield, Duke of Buckingham, frequented Marybone, and at the end of each season gave his companions a dinner with the toast 'May as many of us as remain unhanged next spring meet here again!'. As it turned out, the Duke died in his bed, and was buried in Westminster Abbey.

John Gay's Captain Macheath (1728) says:

There will be deep play tonight at Marybone, and consequently money may be picked up upon the road ... So, Gentlemen, your Servant: You'll meet me at Marybone.[4]

That Marrowbone, Maribone or Marybone, or something similar, was the spelling and probably the pronunciation is clear. In earliest times the settlement was called Tyburn Village, the Tyburn being the twin rivers rising in Hampstead and flowing south towards the Thames. When in 1400 a new church was built opposite the Manor House it was dedicated to St. Mary. The first church had been St. John's, considerably to the south. The village became known as St. Mary-at-Bourne, or St. Mary le Bourne. W. H. Manchée[5] thinks the 'le' might have been introduced by the Huguenots, and confirms that old inhabitants in his day still said 'Marrowbone' or 'Maribone'. Meanwhile, the original name of Tyburn became attached to the district in the west, near the present Marble Arch, and was soon synonymous with the gallows erected there.

Highwaymen and footpads who ended their days at Tyburn continued to be a menace in a sparsely-populated country neighbourhood like Marybone, and the proprietors of the Gardens were obliged to provide armed guards and extra lights.

A charming but possibly apocryphal story describes the sudden appearance of Dick Turpin in the Gardens[6]. He embraced the astonished Mrs. Fountain, one of the visitors, and said 'Madam, have no fear! You can now say you have been embraced by Dick Turpin' and made his escape before she could get her breath back. Dick Turpin was hanged in 1739, so the incident (if it ever took place) must belong to the early years of the Gardens.

As early as 1718 illuminations and a Consort of Music celebrated the birthday of King George I. In 1736 a scaffolding 135 feet high was erected for an acrobatic display in 'the Gardens belonging to the Bowling Green'; a 'Flying Man' was to descend the rope pushing a wheelbarrow, but a high wind blew down the scaffolding and the public was deprived of this interesting spectacle.

In 1737 it was announced that his Royal Highness the Prince of Wales and several 'persons of distinction' would take the Diversion of bowling at Maribone.

Thus amusements at Marybone were gradually becoming more organised, and more genteel, and in the summer of 1737 Daniel Gough, landlord of the Rose Tavern since 1732, 'opened' his Gardens, probably inspired by Jonathan Tyers' example at Vauxhall in 1732.

The story that follows shows how he and his successors fared for the next forty years or so. Their problems and their achievements must be seen against the background of social and topographical change. When Daniel Gough began his venture 'Marybone Town', as the north end of Marylebone Lane was called (now Marylebone High Street), was little more than a country lane meandering up from the Oxford Road to the farms in the Great Park; there was no barrier between the village and that Park. In 1756 the New Road from Paddington to Islington changed this, but for many years the road was only marked by a fence. By the end of the century, however, Marybone's view of Hampstead and Highgate was blocked by houses, and the site of the Gardens was built upon.

Meanwhile the proprietors of the Gardens had tried to

supply their patrons with most forms of entertainment then fashionable except for equestrianism, for which there was not enough space. There were concerts, miniature operas, balls, fireworks, puppets, a conjuror, a magic lantern, lectures on Shakespeare, refreshments and of course fresh air and tree-lined walks.

Having read so far, the modern reader might be inclined to ask: 'But haven't you forgotten the flowers?' Eighteenth-century Gardens of this type were not famous for their flowers. Trees, yes, and gravel walks, but few flowers. At a certain period in Ranelagh's history there is mention of 'a small parterre of flowers', but such a feature was by no means essential.

But by 1776 the old formula seemed no longer to satisfy the Nobility, Gentry and Public. Perhaps fashions in entertainment were changing. Ranelagh, supported in any case by a wealthier and more fashionable clientèle, just survived into the new century with the help of private parties for clubs. The larger Vauxhall was the longest lived, but by the time of its eventual demise in 1859 it had completely changed its character to suit the new age.

The very shortness of Marybone's life – barely forty years – enables us to concentrate both on the general trend of entertainment and on the changes of fashion within than span. Marybone's story is well rounded, and the Gardens did not outlive their popularity for long.

During this short life they made their mark on the history of entertainment and on the social history of their age, giving much interest and pleasure to those who visited them, and I hope some interest and pleasure to those who read the following chronicles.

Notes to Introduction

1   Dr. Ann Saunders: *Regents Park*, 2nd Edition Revised 1981, Bedford College, London, is not only a scholarly and very readable account of the development of Regents Park from 1086, it also has much information about the rest of Marylebone, and is recommended to anyone interested in the topographical and historical background of Marybone Gardens.
2   Daniel Defoe: *A Tour through England and Wales*, 1724; Letter V.
3   Samuel Sainthill: *Memoranda*, 1659; reproduced in *Gentleman's Magazine*, LXXXIII, p. 524.
4   John Gay: *The Beggar's Opera*, 1728.
5   W. H. Manchée: *Proceedings of the Huguenot Society of London*, Vol. XI, No. 1, 1914–1915.
6   This story is given in Warwick Wroth: *The London Pleasure Gardens of the Eighteenth Century*, 1896, and elsewhere, but I have not traced its origin. Fact or fiction, it shows how Dick Turpin, a rather unpleasant highway robber, was romanticised in popular legend, just as Gay made Macheath into a hero and universal charmer. 'Mrs. Fountain' may have been Dr. Fountain's wife (of whom more later) (see p. 38).

Part One

Daniel Gough
1737–1746

I

1737–1740

Mr. Gough's Tavern and his Gardens; No persons of ill repute admitted; A Choice Band of performers playing the most celebrated Pieces of Music; Two great Double Bassoons

In the summer of 1737 Daniel Gough, landlord of the Rose Tavern, opened his Gardens free, doubtless expecting to recoup expenses by the sale of liquor and other refreshments. Unfortunately, much 'indifferent Company' took advantage of his invitation. More respectable Ladies and Gentlemen, 'highly approving of the Entertainment, and the innocent Amusement of the Place' and desirous of 'contributing to so laudable an Undertaking', prevailed on Mr. Gough 'to charge each Gentleman One Shilling Entrance, this sum to include a Lady'. 'The Prices of Wines and Provisions were publicly affix'd in various Parts of the Garden, to prevent the Imposition of Servants.' Care would be taken that 'no Person of ill Repute should enter the Walks'. Moreover, Gentlemen were requested not to smoke.

Thus Marybone Gardens began their eminently respectable career.

In preparation for the 1738 season it was announced that:

Mr. Gough, having already begun to enlarge and beautify his Gardens, and to build an Orchestra, according to an elegant Plan; and having already engaged a choice Band of performers to play the most celebrated pieces of Musick, presumes to hope that all Lovers and Encouragers of Musical Entertainment will honour him with a Subscription.

The subscriptions would be twelve shillings for the season admitting two, represented by a silver Token, or single tickets for one evening could be obtained for 6d each. The importance of high quality music was established from the very beginning.

Mr. Gough's tavern, the Rose, was on the east side of what was then called Marybone Town, now Marylebone High Street, on the site of the present Nos. 35–37. It was a complex of buildings, including stables where visitors from London might put up their horses. It used to be thought that Mr. Gough's 'Rose' was the later 'Rose of Normandy', to the south on the site of No. 32.[1]. (See map on p. 46.)

What was the location and what the extent of the Gardens, enlarged and beautified by Mr. Gough? It seems that they lay behind and to the north of his Tavern and had once belonged to the old Manor House, which was now a boys' school; they probably included the original Sainthill Garden, as we might call it (see p. 3). There were also several 'pieces or parcels' of gardens adjacent to the old French Huguenot Church, known as the French Gardens. The 1746 Rocque Map (see plate 4) shows the Gardens as they had then developed; the bandstand or 'orchestra' which Gough erected can still be seen among plantations of trees to the north-west, and the old Huguenot Church among the garden plots to the west. To the south two bowling greens are divided from the Gardens by a narrow road. In 1753 the Gardens were further enlarged and their area was then said to be eight acres.

In August 1738 Mr. Gough added to his band 'two Great or Double Bassoons', made by Mr. Stanesby Junior, 'the greatness of whose sound surpass that of any other bass instrument whatever'. The Stanesbys, father and son, were famous makers of bassoons, and Mr. Gough could be justly proud of having two of their instruments in his newly formed orchestra. One of the players would almost certainly have been J. F. Lampe, who had come to London from Germany

in 1725, and made a name for himself as a composer as well
as a bassoon player; his burlesque opera *The Dragon of Want-
ley* had been a great success the year before. The second
bassoon might have been Miller, described by Burney as
'the best bassoon player I can remember'. All the players
were clearly well established professionals, glad to pick up
a job during the summer season when the theatres were shut.
Gough claimed to have engaged 'the best Hands' from the
Opera and the two Theatres to play the eighteen best concertos. 'The two Theatres' were the Patent Houses, the Theatres
Royal Drury Lane and Covent Garden, and the Opera was
the King's Theatre in the Haymarket. It would be interesting
to know what were considered 'the eighteen best Concertos'
in the year 1738.

It would be still more interesting to know more about
Daniel Gough and his background. Not all tavern keepers
had such connections in the musical world, and such a knowledge of music.

II

1741–1743

A new and great Organ, and an 'elegant Room';
A future Bluestocking bathes, breakfasts and dances
at Marybone; Admiral Vernon's victory celebrated;
Singers introduced

By the opening of the 1741 season, planned for 27 April,
Mr. Gough could announce 'Great Alterations and Improve-
ments': 'a new and complete Organ' had been built by Mr.
Bridge, the Orchestra (i.e. bandstand) was 'more handsome
and commodious' and 'an elegant Room', the so-called Great
Room, had been erected for 'the better reception of the Nobility and Gentry', which could accommodate balls and the
occasionally rained-off concert. (This was presumably built
on to the Rose.) The Garden Orchestra, however, remained
the centre of music-making, as it did at Vauxhall. People
were attracted to Marybone by its reputation for pure air,
and they liked to remain out-of-doors for the good of their
health as much as possible. And many wind instruments were
still thought to sound better in the open. This announcement
had the unusual heading of 'Mary-le-bon Gardens'.

Concerts would be nightly, and tickets obtained from Mr.
Gough himself at the Rose; from Mr. Brindley, Bookseller
to His Royal Highness in New Bond Street; at Wills' Coffee
House in Scotland Yard; at the Queen's Head, corner of
Holles Street and the Oxford Road; from Mr. Adams, opti-
cian to His Royal Highness at Charing Cross; and from Mr.
Delandre at Temple Bar. The Royal Highness was Frederick,
Prince of Wales, who never lived to be King, but died in

14

1751, leaving his son to become George III in 1760 on the death of George II. Frederick Prince of Wales was a patron of the arts and of music, and a great supporter of Vauxhall. We have seen that he went to Marybone in the early days; later (in 1748) he visited the Gardens, accompanied by the Princess of Wales and 'several persons of distinction'.

Mr. Bridge's organ was played not only during the evening concerts but also during the Public Breakfasting from 10.0 to 1.0 daily.

Among those who breakfasted at Marylebone, according to Dr. Doran[2], was the future 'Bluestocking', Mrs. Montagu, then a lively young thing as fond of dancing as of study, known as 'Fidget'.

It seems that some of the nobility's balls were held at out-of-town Marybone. Before the dancing commenced the gentlemen took it in turn to draw a fan from a pile which the ladies had thrown upon a table; each kept as his partner the owner of the fan.

According to Dr. Doran, Fidget and her friends would get up early, make their way to the 'Plunging Pool' – possibly the Cold Bath in the vicinity of the Gardens. They took headers into the water and gambolled until they were out of breath, to the dismay of the Duchess of Portland, their chaperone. One morning Fidget breakfasted at Marybone, then sat to Mr. Zincke, a fashionable portrait painter, dressed as Anne Boleyn, such historical costume being fashionable, and went to Vauxhall the same evening. Marriage when she was 23 to a much older man tamed her high spirits.

The dancing, bathing and breakfasting at Marybone suggest an eighteenth-century young lady in her teens. Fidget was born in 1720, and therefore some of the Marybone balls might have been held in Mr. Gough's new Great Room, when she would have been 18.

Dr. Doran's account may be somewhat fanciful, but at least it shows that Marybone was sometimes visited by what were known as 'people of fashion' at a certain period, possibly for health reasons. It was a long way from Mayfair and St. James's, but some members of the aristocracy were moving into the new developments of the Portland and the Portman estates north of the Oxford Road. Some of the residents of the developing Cavendish Square perhaps did not disdain a place of amusement so renowned for its healthy air within walking distance, if they ever deigned to walk. Three-quarters of Cavendish Square had been built by 1745, and the southern end of Harley Street was begun in 1729.

Between these developments and the little hamlet round the church, the Manor House and the Rose, there was still open pasture land, however; the footpath and the carriage road were rough and muddy.

The newly prosperous middle classes and 'superior trades-men' from the City or Holborn, to the east of the Gardens, admittedly frequented Marybone Gardens in greater numbers than 'the Nobility' from the south. They welcomed a place of outdoor entertainment more 'genteel' than the north London Tea Gardens, and when the New Road was opened in 1756 Marylebone became still more accessible.

Social distinctions among those who visited the different Gardens existed, but it must be remembered that none of these places was an exclusive club, like Almack's, for instance. If you could pay the entrance money, were decently dressed and behaved with decorum, you would be admitted whatever your social status.

Vauxhall, as we have seen, was opened in 1732 and, although south of the river, was easily reached by boat from Westminster or Mayfair, and when Westminster Bridge was opened (at the end of 1750) there were good carriage routes. Ranelagh, which would open in 1742, was equally easy to reach by water or land. Both were larger and more ambitious than Marybone. Ranelagh indeed had a 'ton' with which even Vauxhall could not compete; it 'totally beat Vauxhall', as Horace Walpole was to write, and 'everyone' went there. Walpole does not even mention Marybone; it was evidently too 'far out' for him. Marybone was a country cousin, with all the limitations and charm this implied.

Fireworks were introduced at Marybone Gardens as early as 1742. Firework displays and the sister art of the transparency celebrated royal birthdays, marriages, and military or naval victories. Until the fall of Sir Robert Walpole in 1742 there were few victories to celebrate, since he had kept England out of foreign entanglements. Just before the end of this long period of peace Admiral Vernon's taking of Cartagena was celebrated in the summer of 1741 by 'A New Grand Martial Composition of Musick' by J. F. Lampe, the bassoonist. Thereafter themes of naval and military glory, and threats of war, would have considerable influence on musical entertainments.

Until 1744 Marybone's music was almost exclusively instrumental, strange in an age of singers. But in June 1744 'to please those who are fond of vocal music, the two famous Miss Scotts' were advertised to sing every evening 'weather permitting', and henceforth Marybone would have a splendid procession of singers performing vocal music of great variety: ballads, burlettas, serenatas, choruses by Handel, Boyce, Arne, Hook, Arnold and many a lesser name. Many of the songs were reproduced in collections such as 'The New Musical Choice' or something similar, with charming vignettes (see plates 11, 12, 13, 14).

III
1743–1746

Composition of orchestra; Leader and Conductor; Mr. Knerler leads, and Mr. Ferrand plays the Pariton at breakfast time; the '45 does not affect Marybone

The size of the Marybone orchestra and the distribution of its instruments can only be guessed at, and in any case it probably fluctuated with the availability of performers and the finances of the managers. But a rough idea can be gained by comparison with similar orchestras of the same period. For instance, the King's Band consisted of 24–26 instruments from 1710 to 1755, and the Foundling Hospital Handel concerts in 1759 numbered 33.

The basis of an orchestra was the string section, of which an average distribution was four first violins, four second, two violas, two 'cellos and two double basses. The woodwind consisted in pairs of oboes and bassoons; flutes could be used instead of oboes for the top line, and sometimes the same players could play either instrument. After the middle of the century clarinets might replace the oboes, and early clarinettists were often oboe players. The difference in tone colour did not seem important, and there was considerable flexibility allowed in performance. But one or more bassoons – perhaps even double bassoons such as Gough introduced – were essential to sustain the bass part.

The brass was limited to horns and trumpets, the latter essential for martial music. Trombones were specified by Handel, but were not yet in general use.

From time to time Marybone advertisements speak of some special woodwind soloist (e.g. Parke on the oboe), but the scoring would be adapted to suit circumstances, probably by the Conductor.

This gentleman did not wave a baton, but was in charge of preparing the performance and supervising it; he sat at the keyboard giving cues to singers, if any, helping to sustain the bass part and giving the tempo, strongly emphasising the beats of the bar to make this clear to the rest of the orchestra. The keyboard instrument would have been a harpsichord in the early days, supported also by the organ. There was a harpsichord in the Card Room of the Assembly Rooms (see p. 71).

Besides – and occasionally instead of – this keyboard Director the Leader or First Violin controlled the ensemble, like the leader of a string quartet or other chamber music ensemble today. Keyboard control gradually died out, leaving the violinist Leader to develop into the conductor-with-a-baton. But as late as Haydn's visits to London in 1791 and 1794 Haydn is described as 'presiding' at the keyboard while Salomon 'led' the orchestra[3].

Every evening in 1744 Mr. Knerler led the orchestra in concertos and symphonies, and every morning Mr. Ferrand played the Pariton (possibly the Baryton or Viola Paradon) for those who liked a morning stroll and breakfast in the Gardens.

War came near to London in 1745 when Prince Charles Edward landed in the Hebrides on 2 August, but news travelled so slowly that on 3 August Marybone was still advertising its nightly entertainments. It was not until the news that the clans had entered Derby reached London that the capital began to panic, and by then it was November, and the Gardens were in recess.

By the time they re-opened for the 1746 season Culloden had been fought. In June the 'rebels' were tried in Westminster Hall, executed on Tower Hill, and their severed heads set up on Temple Bar.

But Marybone was a long way from Temple Bar, and busy with its own affairs.

Notes to Part One

1   Information about the Rose kindly supplied by Mr. Gilbert Lawrance, who has made a special study of the taverns of Marylebone, and was the first to point out that there were two taverns called the Rose, which had hitherto caused much confusion.
2   Dr. John Doran: *A Lady of the Last Century*, London, 1873.
3   Adam Carse: *The orchestra in the XVIII Century*, Cambridge, 1940.

Part Two

John Trusler
1746–1763

I
1746–1753

Early Years

In 1746 Gough's name as landlord of the Rose disappears from the Rate Books, and is succeeded by that of John Trusler until 1764; from 1749 to 1753 Trusler was joined by John Sherratt; and in 1755–1756 by a Mr. Sweedes. The Trusler régime is one of the most interesting periods of the Gardens' history, but also one of the most confusing, and difficult to chronicle accurately. In the early days John Trusler, a cook from Bath, seems to have kept in the background. Perhaps he carried on with the catering, leaving the entertainment side and what one might call the Public Relations to the professional musicians or to the shadowy John Sherratt from 1749 to 1753, and the equally shadowy 'Mr. Sweedes' from 1755–1756. In 1756 John Trusler emerged as the purveyor of a new kind of catering, assisted by his daughter.

It was a period of change for the Gardens; in 1753 they obtained a Licence, and in 1752–1753 they were not only enlarged but underwent changes in lay-out. Perhaps Trusler was occupied with all this, and waiting for his family to grow up meanwhile: his daughter became active in the catering after 1756, and his son, the Rev. John Trusler, together with Stephen Storace, his future son-in-law, launched a series of English translations of Italian burlettas.

Back to the year 1746: there was certainly a 'Band' in attendance in that season, and there is a detailed account of two balls held on 5 and 15 August:

25

The Gardens will be elegantly illuminated, and the whole Band will perform until three o'clock. The Great Room will be decorated with Elegance and Taste, with several of the best Performers to perform Country Dances, the Whole to be managed with Decorum and Decency. (Provisions provided in the same Way as at the Opera and Ranelagh.) Each Ticket 10s. 6d. which admits two Persons.

Patrons had to pay for 'everything they took from the Sideboard'. The elegant illuminations would consist in 500 extra lights, and a guard of soldiers would protect the Company to and from the Gardens.

A renowned and very attractive singer, Miss Falkner or Faulkner, was engaged for the 1747 season, with Henry Rose as first violin and leader and Mr. Philpot as organist. Miss Falkner was to be a Marybone favourite for the next five years. Dublin-born, but with an English husband, Mr. Donaldson, and numerous admirers, she eventually retired to an 'establishment set up for her by the Earl of Halifax', with her husband's full approval.

A Grand Ball was given as early as 12 May 1747. The 'selected Band' which had played at Ranelagh the season before had been engaged, and would play from eleven o'clock until two. Presumably Ranelagh itself was not yet open, and the select band was free to accept this engagement. This performance seems to have been partly concert. Mr. Rose and others were to play country dances in the Great Room and the Saloon in the Gardens. This Saloon must have been an additional building put up by Mr. Gough or Mr. Trusler, for the benefit of the company on wet or chilly evenings. Judging by Vauxhall, such a structure might have been made of little but canvas stretched over wood. Proper care would be taken to provide the best of eatables (here speaks Mr. Trusler, one feels), but ladies and gentlemen were once more exhorted to pay for what they took from the sideboard. The Gardens would be most elegantly lit with the addition of 1,200 lights, whereas the 1746 ball only claimed 500 extra lights. There would be a guard of soldiers and also 'Peace Officers'. And by order of the subscribers no persons whatsoever would be admitted with 'any offensive weapon'.

Such an order was prudent in an age when a petty quarrel could easily flare up into a formal duel. Lord Coke and Sir Harry Bellenden fought in Marybone Fields the following summer, and a few years later two gentlemen fought with swords in the Gardens themselves. In November 1760 George Townshend challenged Lord Albemarle, and off they went to Marybone Fields, but the Captain of the Guard at St. James's followed in a hackney coach, took them back to London in custody, and informed the King, who ordered an enquiry and a reconciliation. (This is a titbit of gossip from Horace Walpole's letters.) Marybone Fields were a good rendezvous for duels, but the Gardens themselves were fairly orderly. (It is true that the Rev. John Trusler, of whom more hereafter, gave a fairly explicit account of the Duke of Cumberland's behaviour in the dark walks, adding that to 'relate it would disgust the reader'.[1])

The next year, 1748, the Dutch-born composer and violinist, William De Fesch, or Defesch as he was more often called in England, was in charge of the music, and wrote music of all kinds for Marybone. A topical song for singers and orchestra was 'in honour of the end of the war with France', to words by Mr. Boyce, a minor poet. The verses were hardly conciliatory:

> Ye Britons to Conquest pursue
> The Trumpet's uplifted for you
> And bid the bold cannon roll
> Thunder to France!

There were more balls, at which full dress was obligatory; there were public breakfastings; there were concerts at which Miss Falkner sang songs by Handel, Mr. Davis played the German flute, Signor Caruso the violin, Mr. Ferrand the Pariton, and the orchestra was led by Mr. Defesch.

Mr. Baker, apparently a tenor, was engaged for the 1749 season. 'At the desire of His Excellency the French Ambassador's wife' there was a Benefit for Miss Falkner at which she and Mr. Baker sang a cantata by John Stanley and a duet from Handel's *Samson*, and various other solos and duets. The instrumental music included concertos on the Violincello (*sic*), the Hautboy, the Organ and the German Flute, played respectively by Messrs. Cervetto, Eiffert, Philpot and Davis. Cervetto, the elder, had come to England in 1728 as cellist, composer and dealer in musical instruments, and for many years had been a leader at Drury Lane, where he was affectionately known as 'Nosey' to the Gallery. Most of the soloists at Marybone were distinguished exponents of their respective instruments. Mr. Defesch published 'Six New Songs', two of which were sung by Miss Falkner at Marybone. Public breakfastings continued on Tuesdays and Fridays. Subscriptions could be obtained from Mr. Montgomery, the Goldsmith of Golden Square.

1749 was the year in which the Peace of Aix-la-Chapelle was publicly celebrated with Handel's *Music for the Royal Fireworks* in the Green Park on 17 April. The rehearsal at Vauxhall had attracted huge crowds, and London Bridge was blocked with carriages for three hours. There was also a performance of fireworks at the Duke of Richmond's house on the Thames on 15 May. Marybone could not compete with such magnificence, but the Peace Celebrations certainly gave an impetus to the fashion.

The Gardens opened early in the year, 1 May, and public breakfasting continued twice a week. Miss Falkner remained the most important singer, and Mr. Defesch continued as leader. Miss Linton and Master Phillips also joined the singers that season, which at the request of the subscribers continued until 27 September, with concerts and firework displays.

In 1750 the tenor Thomas Lowe appeared for the first time. He was a favourite with both Handel and Arne for the beauty of his voice, although unfortunately he was not very musical and had difficulty in learning his songs. Yet he managed to be the first singer of 'Rule Britannia' in Arne's *Alfred* at the Prince of Wales' mansion at Cliveden, and also of several of Arne's Shakespeare songs.

Messrs. Defesch and Boyce remained the chief composer and lyric writer, respectively, and provided Miss Linton with a coy 'Miss Patty', and a rather less conventional 'Female Friendship', in which the singer celebrates the comfort given to the bruised female heart by a confidante:

> The am'rous Heart can never break
> That owns a Female Friend.

This was much in the mood of the contemporary Samuel Richardson heroine, and it is probably no coincidence that the many volumes of Richardson's *Clarissa* were given to a susceptible public between 1747 and 1750.

Songs from T. A. Arne's *Henry and Emma* were sung at Marylebone on 16 August 1750; this 'musical drama' had been given at Covent Garden the previous year, not to be confused with the interlude of the same name of 1774. It has become customary to speak of Thomas Augustine Arne as Dr. Arne, at all periods of his life, but the Doctorate was not conferred upon him until 1759 by the University of Oxford, and in Marybone advertisements of 1750 he was plain 'Mr. Arne'.

'Master' Arne (Michael), his son, made his first appearance at Marybone on 5 July 1751, the next year. He was then 10 or 11, and had made a first appearance at a Haymarket concert in 1750. At Marybone he sang for Miss Falkner's benefit on 8 July and for his own on 13 August. This was a 'Select Entertainment' of vocal music with instrumental interludes. There were Italian songs for both singers, also a Scots song apiece – 'The Highland Lassie' and 'The Bonny Broom' – titles very characteristic of the Scots fashion, also a 'New Duetto'. The instrumental music included T.A.

Arne's Overture to *The Judgement of Paris* and Handel's Overture to *Samson*, also a new concerto on the organ by Arne, played by Mr. Philpot, as well as the *Coronation Anthem*. Tickets price three shillings were to be obtained at Mr. Arne's house in Beaufort Buildings, Strand.

At the end of the season on 26 September 1751, there was a Masquerade, and after the Masquerade fireworks, which it was hoped would not incommode the ladies. Fireworks were not as yet such an indispensable a part of a Marybone evening as they were to become in 1772–1774, hence the apologetic tone. As for masquerades, they had been introduced early in the century by Count Heidegger, and quickly became modish, to the delight of the participants and the scandal of the straitlaced. George II, himself a devotee, made Heidegger Master of the Revels, but was obliged to issue a Royal Proclamation against the obvious evils of this form of entertainment, of which the only result seems to have been that it became known as a Ridotto, or even quite simply as a Ball. Some of Marybone's balls may have been masquerades.

Jonathan Tyers had opened Spring Gardens, Vauxhall, with a Ridotto al Fresco in 1732. The Exhibition on the theme of Masquerades at the Museum of London in 1983 gave a comprehensive view of this kind of entertainment. Marybone's contribution was not mentioned since it was inevitably small. The Lisbon earthquake of 1755 was considered to be a manifestation of the wrath of God upon the immorality of the age, including masquerades, and this form of amusement was therefore stopped . . . for a while!

There were musical changes at Marybone in 1752. The Proprietors (in the plural, presumably Messrs. Trusler and Sherratt) increased the size of the Band, engaging several 'Principals' who had played at Vauxhall, and it was planned to increase the vocal strength also. In order to pay for these developments they decided to raise single admissions to one shilling: these had recently been reduced to sixpence. The public protested and the Proprietors gave way, although they said that the concession would cost them £8 a night extra.

At Miss Falkner's Benefit that summer she sang 'A New Italian Song' by Signor Palma, a new cantata by Mr. Arne, and 'by particular desire' 'Eileen Aroon'. Irish songs were almost as popular as Scots. Other singers were a Mr. Wilder, and 'a new Italian Voice', neither of whom seems to have made much impression.

In December 1752 the Music Hall Act was passed. 'Music Hall' in the nineteenth-century sense was of course unknown, but the Act covered 'House, Room, Garden or other Place kept for public dancing, music or entertainment' in the Cities of London or Westminster, or within twenty miles thereof.

Henceforth such places had to be licensed or they would be classed as 'disorderly Houses'. Marybone obtained a Licence for the first year, 1753. When Torre's fireworks were considered a nuisance in 1774, Marybone lost the Licence, and also probably in the year 1754 for some unknown reason. (See Appendix for more information on Licences.) The need for such an Act shows the extent to which Tea Gardens and their like were proliferating.

It was probably the acquisition of the Licence which made it worth while to enlarge the Gardens until they covered over eight acres. There were major changes in the lay-out of the enlarged Gardens to bring them up to date, as will be explained in V.

The Gardens were opened on 26 May 1753. Entertainments were to take place every evening except Sunday. The band had been enlarged, two 'new Voices' had been engaged, 'Persons with Firearms' would escort the Company along the footpath from Cavendish Square, and lights were to be erected on the coachway from the Oxford Road. The Persons with Firearms were not to be given money.

The two new voices were presumably Mrs. Chambers and Mrs. Ramelio. Mrs. Ramelio had an ingratiating 'puff' in the *London Advertiser* of 8 June 1753: 'Utterly unacquainted with the British Style in Singing, and to make herself agreeable' she had been studying those 'divine Performances of English Oratorios all the Winter, and would make her first Appearance with "Return, O God of Hosts" that evening, begging that she might not be judged'. This was an alto aria by Handel, first sung by Mrs. Cibber.

In spite of her studies and her conscientious desire to please, Mrs. Ramelio does not seem to have established herself as a worthy successor to Miss Falkner, who that summer retired to the love nest built for her by Lord Halifax. The other 1753 newcomer, Mrs. Chambers, became a Marybone 'regular'. One of the songs she sang, 'Polly of the Plain', was printed in 1754.

The Proprietors engaged with 'proper Engineers' to make fireworks, and printed an impressive programme of Turbillons, Mortars, Air Balloons, Porcupine Quills, Pyramids and assorted Suns and Stars. According to Donald Garstang, Archivist to Messrs. Colnaghi, it was in 1753 that Giovanni Battista Torre first came to London, and worked with a member of the Brock family in a display at Marybone Gardens, but shortly afterwards left for Paris. Torre's later career at Marybone will be described in Part Four, IV *et seq.*

II

1754-1755

*A Mystery Year; The Rose and the Gardens' lease
for sale; John Trusler asserts himself in 1755*

1754 is a mystery year in the annals of the Gardens. The newspapers are silent. Perhaps there was a complete breakdown in public relations, but this seems unlikely.

A clue may lie in the following advertisement which appeared in one of the public prints in September 1754:

> To be sold to the highest Bidder at the Rose Tavern in Marybone on Wednesday the 11th September between 3 and 4 o'clock in the Afternoon. The Remainder of a Lease which will expire seven Days before Lady Day, 1756, of the said Tavern with its Gardens and Appurtenances, commonly called Marybone Gardens, subject to a yearly rent of £100 pounds 5s 6d. For further Particulars enquire of Joseph Letch in Elm Court, Temple.

The interpretation of this clue, if it can be called such, is not easy. John Trusler had been assessed for the rates since 1746; in 1756, the year when the lease was due to expire, the name of his partner Sweedes alone appears; from 1757–1763, however, Trusler's name stands alone as ratepayer. To add to the confusion, there appeared in the press in May 1755 a rumour to the effect that John Beard, the famous tenor, had taken the Gardens.

The most likely explanation is that Marybone lost its recently acquired Licence in 1754, and that the Gardens were open with no organised entertainment. This happened to

33

Ranelagh in that same year, 1754[2].

But by 1755 both Gardens were functioning normally. Press coverage of 1755 at Marybone is somewhat sparse, but there is evidence of musical and pyrotechnic activity. Important in this context is the paragraph which appeared in *The Public Advertiser* of 4 September 1755:

> Whereas on Tuesday last it was advertised that a grand Collection of Fireworks, with vocal and instrumental Musick, would be performed at this Place on this day *on the Failure of our Success in America* I beg leave to assure the Publick that this unprecedented Advertisement was published in direct Opposition to my Persuasions and Advice, by a Person who assumed the Character of an Agent to my Partner.

> 'As I am truly sensible, that to make any Misfortune of one's Country the Subject of Public Diversion and Amusement is a very great and inexcusable Offence; I take this Method of expressing my Dislike and Abhorrence thereof; and will do every Thing in my Power to put a Stop to a Thing of this Nature; I therefore humbly Hope that I shall bear no Part of the public Censure or Resentment.
>
> JOHN TRUSLER

Some military setback in the early days of the war in America must have been the subject of the entertainment. Sweedes seems to have been his 'partner' at this time.

The above paragraph is signed boldly and unequivocally JOHN TRUSLER, although his partner, Sweedes, had been assessed for that year. Thereafter Sweedes' name disappears.

The *Public Advertiser* announced a benefit for Mr. Thornton on 11 and 12 September, consisting of vocal and instrumental music, followed by 'an extraordinary Display' of Chinese and Italian Fireworks, including 'several Transparent Machines and Illuminations of Slow Fire, with Fire Pumps, &c., &c.'.

III

1756–1757

John Trusler and his family; Catering in the best Manner

The sparseness of press coverage in the early years of the Trusler reign was amply compensated for in 1756 and later. Advertisements show a new emphasis on catering and on the home grown produce which gave the catering its special character.

Two large refreshment rooms 'genteely fitted-up' were to be let for private balls, public dinners, etc., and the Proprietor, 'being a Cook', would cater for any such entertainment 'in the best manner':

> Gentlemen and Ladies who shall favour him with their Company may depend upon the best of all kinds of Provisions and Liquors as reasonable as at any other Place; and that to please and give Satisfaction will be the constant Study and endeavour of their most obedient and humble Servant, JOHN TRUSLER.

The 'elegant New Room' erected by Gough in 1739–1740 must have been enlarged. As well as being able to give parties at Marybone, visitors could enjoy daily entertainment and refreshment:

> Gentlemen and Ladies may every Morning breakfast on Tea, Coffee and Chocolate, with the finest Butter, Cream and new Milk, Cows being kept for that Purpose; and Afternoons and Evenings be entertained with Coffee, Tea, Cakes, Pastry and all sorts of Wines and other Liquors.

John Trusler was assisted in the catering and cooking by

35

'Miss Trusler'. Most writers assume this lady to have been Elizabeth, the eldest daughter, who married Stefano Storace in 1751, but the present writer thinks that Mary, the second daughter, is more likely to have been the caterer[3].

A rare print in the Harvard Theatre Collection (plate 10), dated 1760 by the experts, shows Miss Trusler as a plump young lady sitting in an armchair holding a glass of (presumably) brandy in her right hand; in front of her is a counter or sideboard upon which is what looks like a pastry tart or pie. Below is the verse:

> 'Sov'reign of Cates, all hail! Nor thou refuse
> This cordial off'ring from an English Muse
> Who pours the brandy in Libation free
> And finds Plumb Pudding realiz'd in Thee!'

In the 'Schedule of Appointments' made in 1768 at the time of Thomas Lowe's bankruptcy we read of the catering equipment as: 30 mahogany tea-boards, 30 black teapots and cream pots, 74 garden table cloths, and 74 cruet stands, as well as an ample supply of forks, knives and spoons, and 22 punch bowls with ladles.

Staton's Tea House 'opposite Marybone Gardens' was clearly less ambitious than the Gardens' own catering, and probably also less expensive:

> Ladies and Gentlemen may be served with either fine Tea, Coffee or Chocolate with French Roll and Butter at 6d each person any hour of the Day. Neat Wines &c. Dinners &c dressed at reasonable prices.

IV
1758–1759

Burlettas and Sermons; Storace and young Trusler;
The Manor House School; Dr. and Mrs. Fountain

But Marybone Gardens were more than an outdoor eating house. Regular concerts continued, and in 1758 a series of burletta performances was inaugurated, which had considerable importance in English musical history.

At this period and in this context a burletta was a kind of miniature comic opera, for a small number of characters. The first of these burlettas to be given at Marybone was an English translation of Pergolesi's *La Serva Padrona* (*The Maid and Mistress*), which had already been performed in Italian at the Haymarket in March 1750. Giovanni Battista Pergolesi (1710–1736) had originally written *La Serva Padrona* as an Intermezzo; its two acts were given during the two intervals of a serious opera also written by Pergolesi. But the Intermezzo became immensely popular in its own right, and the serious opera was forgotten. In course of time the operatic convention which required an Intermezzo was also forgotten.

La Serva Padrona was tuneful, amusing and needed only two singers; the simple plot tells us how Serpina the servant lures her old master into marrying her. It remains popular all over Europe. At Marybone a third character was sometimes introduced.

On 8 June 1758 it appeared at Marybone in English as *The Servant Mistress*, translated from the Italian by Stefano

37

Storace, better known as Stephen, and John Trusler Junior. Storace was born about 1725 at Torre Annunziata near Naples, and by 1748 was working in Dublin as a professional musician. He was a fine double-bass player and an all-round musician. The elder Sheridan engaged him for his band at the Smock Alley Theatre, and he ran the music at Dublin's New Gardens and Johnson's Music Hall. By the time he came on the Marybone scene he could write good English, as is shown by a letter he wrote to the *Gentleman's Magazine* about the Tarantula in September 1753.

John Trusler Junior, his collaborator, was born in London somewhere about 1735, and educated until the age of 15 at Westminster; he then went to Dr. Fountain's celebrated school for young gentlemen in Marylebone's Old Manor House, from whence he proceeded to Emmanuel College, Cambridge; he took his B.A. the year before the collaboration.

The Old Manor House had been turned into a school for young gentlemen in 1703 by Mr. de la Place; he was succeeded by Dr. Fountain who married de la Place's daughter, Jane Anne. There are many descriptions of the school from former pupils, notably by J. T. Smith in *A Book for a Rainy Day*. At one time there were about 100 boys, who walked two by two to church on Sundays, some in pea green, some in sky blue and some in scarlet. Dr. Fountain was a kindly old scholar known as Bushwig. His wife was a more enigmatic character, known as Rainbow from her dyed hair, described by some as 'a sweet woman' and reputed to be very kind to the younger boys, bribing them to do their lessons with milk and biscuits. On the other hand, she was accused of taking favourite scholars to the play, and charging the parents with the price of the tickets which she obtained free. And she was accused of being a 'climber' and a snob[4].

This original character will reappear in 1772 as 'Mrs. Fountain who keeps a boarding school (for young ladies) near the Gardens' protesting against the fireworks. In 1741 a

Plate 1. Marybone Gardens by John Donowell, detail of left side.

Plate 2. Marybone Gardens by John Donowell, detail of centre.

Plate 3. Marybone Gardens by John Donowell, detail of right side.

Plate 4. Section of John Rocque's Map of London, 1746.

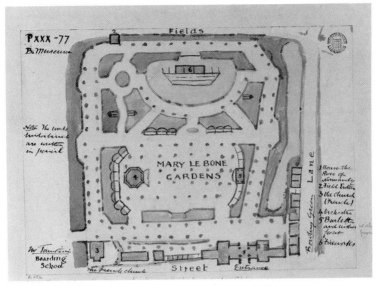

Plate 5. The Crace Plan, 1756.

Plate 6. The Field Entrance to Marybone Gardens by J. T. Smith,
'drawn of memory'.

Marybone Turnpike

Plate 7. View from Marybone Turnpike, looking south to the Manor House, behind which lay the Gardens, by Samuel H. Grimm, 1772

Plate 8. View from Marybone Turnpike, looking north over what is now Regent's Park, by Samuel Hieronymous Grimm.

For the Benefit of the WAITERS.

THE most celebrated ARTIST, whose abilities have deservedly recommended him to the public in an uncommon degree, will exhibit at MARYBONE-GARDENS, THIS EVENING, Sept. 10, an exceedingly beautiful and elegant

FIREWORK.

Before the Firework will be

A CONCERT;

In the course of which an Entertainment of Music, called

THE MAGNET,

Will be sung by Mr. Bannister, Mrs. Forbes, and Mrs. Thompson. The other vocal parts by Mr. Culver and Mrs. Cartwright.

A new favourite Song by Mrs. Cartwright.
"With Horns and with Hounds," by Mrs. Thompson.
Several favourite Songs by Mrs. Forbes.
New Musical Imitations by Mr. Bannister.
Concerto Organ by Mr. Hook.

For that night only, the Gardens will be most elegantly illuminated in a new and curious manner, with many thousand Lamps.

Admittance 2s. 6d. each.

Tickets sold in the fields or streets leading to the Gardens will not be admitted, as there will be proper persons to prevent the same.

SIGNOR TORRE

WILL exhibit Tomorrow, Friday, September 11, (for the second, and last time but one of his performing this season) at

MARYBONE GARDENS,

A most uncommon and exceedingly magnificent

FIREWORK,

Which will conclude with a Representation of HERCULES delivering THESEUS from HELL, In the Course of this Exhibition some very curious and beautiful pieces will be introduced; and before it will be a CONCERT of Vocal and Instrumental

MUSIC.

The Vocal Parts by Mr. Bannister, Mr. Culver, Mrs. Forbes, Mrs. Cartwright, and Mrs. Thompson.

Admittance Two Shillings and Six-pence.

The Firework will begin punctually at half past nine.

Plate 9. Fireworks and Music. An advertisement of 10 September 1772

Library had been built to house the Harleian Collection just 'behind the Manor House' where Dr. Fountain had his school for young gentlemen. But when Lord Harley died, the same year, it became a girls' school. This in all probability was Mrs. Fountain's boarding school. The Crace Plan (see plate 5) identifies *Mr.* Fountain's boarding school as next to the little French Church, with its frontage on the High Street, which certainly makes it 'near the Gardens', and within reach of falling rockets, and could apply to either school.[5].

It is curious that in such a class-ridden age young Trusler, son of a pastry cook, should have been accepted at the Manor School. He was certainly a brilliantly clever boy, but there were no scholarships at such schools in those days. Perhaps young Trusler was allowed to enter the school when his father took up residence near by.

The year after his appearance at Marybone, collaborating in *La Serva Padrona*, he was ordained; he held various curacies, and wrote at least one famous book, *Hogarth Moralised*. He also produced a book of sermons for the use of preachers too lazy or too stupid to produce their own; this was in script characters which the congregation might suppose was the preacher's own writing.

In 1766 he advertised that he would 'perform' Divine Service in the Marylebone church. This was the church built in 1742 which replaced that which can be seen in Number V of 'The Rake's Progress', pulled down when Trusler was a child. This church in its turn was pulled down in 1948, but its site is clearly marked by a memorial garden.

John Trusler's later career has carried us ahead of the first Marybone performance of *La Serva Padrona*. The collaboration between the professional musician from Southern Italy and the somewhat eccentric but serious-minded son of the Bath cook was apparently satisfactory, although Trusler claims all the credit, and does not even mention Storace as having any share in the enterprise in his *Memoirs* of 1806. (Nor does he allude to his father being a 'cook' and his sister following the same occupation) The *Memoirs* indeed are ego-centric. (See Note 1 *supra*.)

We have independent evidence of the collaboration, and this led to some recrimination, as will be seen. The performance was highly successful, the music 'directed' by Storace, and had nearly 70 performances in the first season, and many revivals in subsequent years, including one at the Haymarket Theatre. The singers were Signorina Saratina, an Italian, and Frederick Charles Reinhold, English-born bass and organist of German extraction, who was at Marybone for several seasons and well known in oratorio and English opera. Handel's bass parts suited his voice, and 'O ruddier than the Cherry' from *Acis and Galatea* was one of his most famous 'pieces'.

The introduction of burlettas necessitated the erection of a small theatre, of which more will be said in the next chapter.

Meanwhile, back to 1759: Storace translated two more burlettas for Marybone without the help of young Trusler – *La Stratagemma*, attributed to Pergolesi, and *Il Cicisbeo alla Moda* (*The Modish Coquet*), attributed to Baldassare Galuppi.

1759 was not merely a good year for Marybone's music – it was the Wonderful Year for British victories, for which Dr. William Boyce wrote 'Heart of Oak'. This rejoicing in feats of arms did not please everybody. Horace Walpole looked back with nostalgia to the days when his father had kept England at peace.

The Gardens were open for breakfasting, with Miss Trusler's renowned plum and seed cakes on sale. Sir John Fielding, the magistrate, said that 'doubtful' places of entertainment such as Mrs. Cornelys' in Soho Square were unnecessary when there were so many other attractions in London, such as Ranelagh with music and fireworks, and Marybone with music, wine and plum cake.

As many people had expressed a desire to sup in the Gardens and not merely partake of light refreshments, boxes had been 'enclosed' and 'little Rooms' very convenient for the purpose had been set aside. Such new arrangements suggest assignations as well as supper, but Marybone's reputation was in general good.

*The Gardens in the mid-eighteenth century; The
Donowell View and the Crace Plan; The New Road;
Changes in Marylebone*

As has already been briefly mentioned, there had been a
major change in the lay-out of the Gardens when they were
enlarged in 1752–1753. What was left of the old Sainthill
design disappeared when the central Bowling Green was
absorbed into the general design. Its square had been previously surrounded by a circular walk. The existing Walks
were thereby rendered 'more commodious', and new straight
Walks were added.

'Several thousand' (!) more trees were planted, and the
Gardens 'enlightened' with a great number of lights. This
was to be a Garden of tree-lined Walks and vistas, an attempt
to emulate Vauxhall and Ranelagh. Clearly the money did
not run to statues, but a Temple was introduced. This 'feature' caused the Proprietors some annoyance; a 'Foreigner'
had promised to make a cascade and other 'Orniments' (probably in imitation of the cascade at Vauxhall) but failed to
carry out his promise. However, the Temple itself remained,
and was later adorned with busts of Shakespeare and Handel.

Imaginary tours of Vauxhall and Ranelagh are comparatively easy, because there are so many pictures as well as
verbal descriptions to help us. They attracted a larger and
a wealthier clientèle than Marybone, and there was a big
demand for the equivalent of picture postcards for visitors
to take home. It was worthwhile commissioning artists and

producing prints.

Alas, no Canaletto or Samuel Wale visited Marybone, and we have only one View, admittedly a very charming one, allegedly painted in 1755 and reproduced many times thereafter with various modifications. The number of these reproductions shows that there was a certain demand for pictures of Marybone.

John Donowell was a well known architect, and exhibited drawings and designs for country houses between 1778 and 1786, some of which were published as engraved prints. But no watercolour other than the 'View of the Grand Walk at Marybone' has been attributed to him, and nothing is known of his life.

The 'View', No. 25 in the J. Leslie Wright Bequest at the City of Birmingham Museum and Art Gallery, is in watercolour and pen over pencil, on white laid paper, and measures 24.4 × 40.8 cm. On the verso is inscribed 'Nath. Smith', who presumably commissioned the work, and lower down we read what he paid for it: £2.2.0 for the View and 15s. od for the figures. (See plates 1, 2, 3 and cover.)

The colouring of the original is delicate and subdued, possibly faded and possibly added by another hand. It would be almost impossible to reproduce. A gentleman in a scarlet coat to the right of the picture, balanced by another to the left, contrasts with ladies, whose gowns are mostly soft blue.

There is no date beside the signature, but 1755 is the date assigned by the Crace Collection in the British Library.

We are in the centre of the Gardens looking westward towards the High Street entrance and frontage. The Grand Walk, slightly to the left of centre, seems to stretch to infinity, and in the distance can be seen the parish church of St. Mary's, where young Trusler was to 'perform' Divine Service in 1766. In the middle distance the Grand Walk has an archway, which looks like wrought iron, but might be wood, hung with lamps, and there are lamps attached to the trees. In the middle distance can also be seen some trellises, probably

43

supper boxes. On each side of the Grand Walk is a slightly narrower walk, also tree-lined. The tall trees, difficult to identify, have been shorn of their lower branches, so that the scene is open on ground level, with a leafy canopy above.

Framing the picture on either side, and facing each other, are the two buildings: the Orchestra on our right, and the Burletta Theatre on our left. In the centre foreground is an elderly couple, evidently of importance to artist or patron. Dare we identify them with Dr. and Mrs. Fountain?

The other ladies and gentlemen are young and elegant. This seems the very centre of the Gardens' social life, of meetings and greetings, on a fine evening in high summer. Later these charming people will listen to the concert, visit the Burletta Theatre, sup and watch fireworks.

It is sad to think that this should be Donowell's only View of the kind. Since he was primarily an architect we expect the vistas and the buildings to be convincing, but the groups of ladies and gentlemen standing around and the glimpses of musicians with their instruments make up such a lively human scene that we wish for more eighteenth-century views of Marybone or elsewhere.

The Crace Plan, dated 1756 (plate 5) shows the Gardens as rectangular, with the High Street as the base of the rectangle. They are viewed the other way up from the Donowell 'View'. From left to right along the High Street, Mrs. Fountain's Boarding School and the French Chapel are named, and then there are various unnamed buildings until we come to the 'Rose' entrance, about three-quarters of the way along the frontage. The Burletta Theatre and the Orchestra face each other across what was once probably the central bowling green. Both Warwick Wroth in *London Pleasure Gardens of the Eighteenth Century* and George Clinch in *Marylebone and St. Pancras* call the building facing the Orchestra 'The Great Room', although they both knew the Crace Plan. I stick to the Crace identification and to my view that 'The Great Room' ('Long Room', 'Elegant New Room', 'Assembly Room', etc.) was an integral part of 'The Rose'. 'The Rose' was a complex of buildings, as we know, and the Crace Plan shows this along the High Street frontage.

Continuing eastwards, towards the top of the rectangle, we come to a semi-circular area for viewing fireworks and the fireworks building itself. Continuing to the north-east, we are shown the Field Entrance (plate 6), and beyond that ... just fields.

We must allow for the fact that the Donowell View is probably romanticised, and the Crace Plan not to scale. Deduction, and admittedly guesswork and imagination, play their part in a mental picture of the Gardens.

Still more difficult is it to identify the exact site of any particular feature on a modern map. The late eighteenth-century development was on a different axis, and a grid plan, as is shown by the map on p. 46.

But two landmarks remain to remind us of the outline of the Gardens: the gentle curve of the High Street itself, far older than the Gardens, and a short stretch of Weymouth Street as far as Beaumont Street, once Bowling Green Alley.

Meanwhile Marylebone itself was undergoing major changes during the Trusler period. In 1757 'the new Road from Paddington to Islington was begun – now Marylebone Road, Euston Road and Pentonville Road. This made a new link between Essex and Middlesex. The army could reach the coast in time of national emergency without going through the cities of London and Westminster, and cattle could be driven direct to Smithfield Market without going along the Oxford Road.

In the long run this road would cut Marylebone off from the open pasture land (now Regents Park), sloping north-wards to the heights of Hampstead, making it less rural. The handsome houses to be built along the New Road would block for ever the country view, and make Marylebone a more integral part of London than it had been. People would look south, rather than north. But for ten years or so the view was blocked only by a post-and-rail fence to define the roadway along which processions of cattle made their way to Smithfield, and the occasional coach and horses passed (plates 7 and 8). Access to the Gardens was easier from the City than it had been before. It was not until the end of the century, by which time the Gardens had disappeared, that the great changes brought about by the New Road to this part of London became apparent.

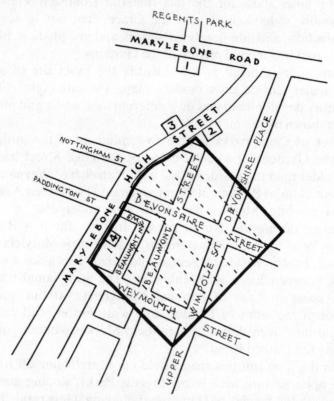

The site of Marylebone Gardens, imposed on the present street pattern.
1. The present Marylebone Church, 1819.
2. The Manor House, demolished 1791.
3. Site of old Marylebone Church, demolished 1948.
4. Main entrance to Marylebone Gardens, and site of the Rose tavern.

VI

1760–1761

Fresh mincepies daily; Miss Trusler offers help with home catering; Dispute between Trusler and Storace; Trusler-Storace marriage

Although the Gardens were a place of summer entertainment, during the Trusler régime (at least from 1760 to 1761) they were open for 'genteel Company' through the winter months. No amusements were provided, but Mince Pies of the very best were made fresh daily, which must have been an attraction on a cold day.

Miss Trusler enlarged her menu in 1760, and also offered to help with home catering:

Miss Trusler begs Leave to inform the Nobility and Gentry that she intends to make Fruit Tarts during the Fruit Season; and hopes to give equal Satisfaction as with the rich Cakes and Almond Cheese-cakes. The Fruit will always be fresh-gathered, having great Quantities in the Garden, and none but Loaf Sugar used and the finest Epping Butter. Tarts of a twelvepenny Size will be made every Day from One to Three O'Clock; and those who want them of larger Size to fill a Dish are desired to speak for them, and send their Dish or the Size of it, and the Cake shall be made to fit. The Almond Cheese-cakes will be always hot at One o'Clock as usual, and the rich Seed and Plum Cakes sent to any Part of the Town at 2s6d each (*Public Advertiser*, 6 May 1760).

In the summer of 1760 there was a dispute between Stephen Storace and the Truslers concerning the 'Books' (i.e. Libretti) of the Burlettas. The *Public Advertiser* of 2 August

47

carried this notice:

> Whereas the Master of Marylebone Gardens had thought proper to publish the following Paragraph:
>> The genuine Books of the Burlettas to be had of Mrs. Trusler at the Bar of the Gardens. All sold about the Door or elsewhere being wrong . . .
>
> (Besides a Person being employed to caution everybody not to buy any of my Books).
> This is to assure the Public that the Books of the several Burlettas sold at the Door are the same Books that have been performed there, and those sold at the Bar are Copies pirated from me, which (contrary to Agreement) have been re-printed in order to deprive me of the Advantage which (by Contract) I was to have, I being the Author and Inventor of all the Burlettas there performed.
>
> STEPHEN STORACE

By 'Author and Inventor' he presumably meant of the respective Libretti, but doubtless in eighteenth-century fashion he adapted the music also to suit the circumstances, the singers and his own taste. Accusations of 'piracy' were not easily made 'to stick' in the eighteenth century.

However, the Storace–Trusler dispute was somehow patched up, for in the following year Stephen Storace married Elizabeth Trusler on 16 June 1761. Two exceptionally talented children were born to them: Stephen on 4 April 1762, and Anna Selina ('Nancy') on 27 October 1765. Stephen was a very gifted composer, who became a friend and possibly pupil of Mozart in Vienna, and died at the age of 32 and was buried in Marylebone Church near the Gardens, where his uncle, John Trusler, had preached. Nancy was Mozart's first Susanna in *The Marriage of Figaro* (Vienna, 1786), and had a long career in London subsequently. Except for Stephen Storace's grievance over the Burletta Libretti, 1760 seems to have been a prosperous year: the Gardens opened on 11 May, when all 'genteel Parties' could be accommodated with Chocolate in the morning, with Tea (and organ music) from five o'clock, and later in the evening there would be concerts and/or one of the above mentioned Burlettas.

In the summer of the Storace–Trusler wedding there was also a Royal Wedding – George III to Charlotte of Mecklenburg-Strelitz – and also a Coronation (George II having died the previous October).

VII

1762

'Much the pleasantest Place about Town'; 'No improper Company'; The Summer of the Chiefs; End of the Trusler Régime

Fireworks and concerts continued during 1762, but the publicity emphasis was on the charms of the Gardens as a place of recreation, where the beauties of nature could be enjoyed, and also good quality refreshments, especially in the morning.

'Marybone Gardens is by much the pleasantest place about Town (the new City Road leading to it and being a pleasant airing), is now in perfect good Order, the Trees in full Leaf and the Shrubs in full Bloom, which renders them more immediately sweet and refreshing in the Morning, and their being so near Town are thought by most of the Nobility and Gentry to be very commmodious for breakfasting at. Mr. Trusler to make them more so will take care that no improper Company will be admitted, and the very best Tea, Coffee, Cream, Butter, etc., may be depended on as usual.' Milk, cream and butter were from the Truslers' own cows, of course. On one occasion, they advertised for 'A clean Servant that can milk'. 'They are open every Evening when Wine, Tea, Cakes, etc., may be had.'

It may be noticed that the Shrubs would be in full bloom; what the shrubs were we do not know, but this is the first and probably the only time when anything in the nature of a bloom was mentioned.

In 1762 London in general and Marybone in particular
had a rare opportunity to see in the flesh some inhabitants
of our American Colonies: 'the Cherokee King and two
Chiefs' or 'the Four Indian Chiefs and their Ladies'; the press
differed as to the exact number and composition of the party.
By their own account they were Chiefs of the five tribes
of Iroquois Indians whose homeland was 'between New York
and Lake Ontario'. Accompanied by Henry Timberlake and
Thomas Sumter, they had come to complain to King George
III that a great part of their land had been taken from them
by 'Persons from New York'. His Majesty received them
graciously, but whether they had any other satisfaction than
this gracious reception seems doubtful.

They were welcomed at places of entertainment in London. At Vauxhall they became drunk, but at Marybone their
behaviour seems to have been more decorous. They stayed
in Marylebone 'for the sake of the air' at the house of Thomas
Lowe, the singer, and dined in public in the Gardens in a
specially fitted up box. Visitors were admitted at 6d a head.

The men were at least six feet tall, dressed in shirt, trousers
and mantle, their heads adorned with shells, feathers and
earrings, and their faces painted a copper colour. Oliver
Goldsmith called upon them, and they were so grateful for
some 'trifle' he had given them that they suddenly embraced
him, and transferred much of their paint to his face[6] They
were 'very affable, humane Sort of People', and their ladies
'very modest and decent in their behaviour'. There were
nightly concerts of vocal and instrumental music (no performers named) so that the Chiefs must have listened to some
(to them) strange sounds. A second visit to Marybone
included Fireworks 'By Order of the Indian Chiefs and their
Ladies' specially designed by Mr. Clitherow to celebrate the
birth of a Prince of Wales. They had already seen some fireworks and also equestrian displays at the Star and Garter
Tavern, Chelsea.

After what must have been a very exciting visit, the Chiefs

and their ladies set off for Portsmouth, and sailed for home in the 'Epreuve'.

The Summer of the Chiefs, 1762, was to be the last Trusler season at the Gardens. Presumably the whole family moved with 'Miss Trusler' to the Gold Lamp, Boyle Street, the upper end of Savile Row, but when the move took place we do not know. In 1766 she was advertising the usual Seed and Plum Cakes, adding various other delights such as 'Tanseys of any Size garnished with Orange', 'a Dish called a Trifle which is exceeding good', Syllabubs and Jellies. Fine Epping Butter was sold in Pats, at 2d a Pat. Orders could be sent by the Penny Post. Most of us think of the Penny Post as the 'invention' of Rowland Hill, but there had been a local postal service in London since 1680, which in some central areas provided twelve deliveries a day. Miss Trusler also advertised dried apples and pears, and stewed apples. Perhaps she still used fruit from Marybone Gardens.

It is tempting to follow the catering theme, but it takes us too far from our main subject. It is to be hoped that the West End of London was ready for this gourmet food, which was perhaps too expensive for Marybone patrons.

Storace and the former Elizabeth Trusler continued to live in Marylebone, and he translated and arranged more Burlettas for performance.

Meanwhile the Gardens were taken over by Thomas Lowe, the tenor, who had already sung in the concerts, and at whose house the Indian Chiefs had stayed.

Notes to Part Two

1 *Memoirs* of the Rev. John Trusler (quoted in a scrapbook at the Royal College of Music also in Warwick Wroth: *The London Pleasure Gardens of the Eighteenth Century*, and elsewhere). Part I was published in Bath, 1806.

2 Dr. Ann Saunders in her *Regents Park* (*op. cit*) says that Dr. Arne was appointed 'resident composer and music master' during this 'mystery year'. I can find no corroboration of this, although Arne made personal appearances at various later dates, and his music was frequently performed at Marybone, as elsewhere.

3 Mr. Geoffrey Brace, who has made a special study of the Storace family, agrees with me.

4 Dr. and Mrs. Fountain, Fountaine or Fountayne; the spelling varies. Fountain is used throughout this book. Background information about this couple can be found in: J. T. Smith: *A Book for a Rainy Day*, 1845; Wilfred Whitten edition, 1903, p. 44; J. T. Smith: *Nollekens and his Times*, 1828; William Hone: *Yearbook*, 1838 (under 23 April); W. H. Manchée, see Note 5 of Introduction; John Colman the Younger: *Random Records*, 1830.

5 The French or 'old Huguenot Church' almost faced the end of Paddington Street, and may have been originally an outbuilding of the Rose. It was used by the congregation of Huguenot refugees formed in 1685, and still used in 1754, as is shown by an advertisement for the 'French Boarding School for Young Ladies', which drew special attention to the fact that there were 'exceeding good pews for young Ladies, both in the English and French Churches at Mary-le Bon' (*Public Advertiser*, Saturday, 15 June *et seq*, 1754). This French Boarding School had no connection with that of Mrs. Fountain, as far as can be ascertained.

6. John Forster: *Life of Oliver Goldsmith*, 1848.

Part Three

Thomas Lowe
1763–1768

I

1763

Lowe and Storace; The Guard for Foot passengers;
Ann Catley and other singers; Handel at Marybone

John Trusler was still paying rates in 1763, and did not move
from Marylebone until 1764, when he seems to have gone
to Boyle Street, Savile Row. He died at his house in Savile
Row on 2 April 1766. Thomas Lowe, however, 'managed'
the Gardens from their opening in May 1763, and his status
was confirmed by a 14-year Lease granted by Robert Long,
of the Bowling Green, at £170 per annum. Robert Long had
paid rates on the 'Bowling Green and Garden' for many
years. In addition he had evidently bought the lease from
Daniel Gough of the Rose Tavern, the old French Chapel
and the so-called Great Garden, with 'several pieces or parcels of garden ground', the orchestra, and rooms and buildings erected thereupon, and must have granted a lease to
Trusler also. It is because of Lowe's bankruptcy, presumably,
that the Inventory of his lease has been preserved[1].

J. T. Smith describes Lowe about this time riding in his
'chariot', with a large tin trunk behind him in which he
planned 'to place the profits from the Gardens'[2].

'The Apotheosis of Thomas Lowe' (plate 17) shows a more
than life-sized Apollo descending to earth on a solid cloud,
his right hand holding a lyre and his left pointing at Thomas
Lowe, a slim young man with a chubby face in elegant mid-
eighteenth-century attire. The background shows a woodland
scene, and the foreground is filled in with a rococo deco-
ration.

57

Early in the season the world was told that the Gardens would be

Open every Evening during the Summer Season with a Concert of vocal and instrumental Music. On rainy Evenings the Concert will be in the Long Room in the House.

Mr. Lowe and Mr. Storace acquaint the Public that for the Greater Security of Ladies and Gentlemen who shall honour them with their Company they have doubled the Guard on the Road and in the Fields. They are stationed within Call of each Other from the Gardens to the Oxford Road for Coaches, and from the Field Gate of the Gardens to Harley Street, Cavendish Square, for Foot Passengers.

There is a Guard appointed to escort Foot Passengers also to Paddington, which will set out regularly from the Gardens as soon as the performance is finished at the stated Hours of Eleven and Twelve.

'The Long Room in the House' was almost certainly another name for Gough's 'elegant New Room', 'the Assembly Room', etc. It was usual for a tavern to boast a Long Room; in course of time the entertainments given in the Long Room became the genesis of the nineteenth-century Music Hall. Our Rose never saw the nineteenth century, but its namesake (on the site of No. 32) did become quite a famous Music Hall, which has caused a certain amount of confusion among local historians until Mr. Gilbert Lawrance's researches distinguished between the two taverns called the Rose (see Note 1, Notes to Part One).

Storace's name is associated with that of Lowe on equal terms. It is probable Storace helped to 'conduct' (in the eighteen-century sense) the more ambitious programmes, at least. Having been in charge of the music at Johnson's Music Hall and the New Gardens, Dublin, he must have been experienced in arranging concerts. He may even have 'directed' such performances from the keyboard; this would not have been unusual for a string player. The First Violin (and therefore Leader) seems to have been Signor Rodrigo at this period. All-round musicianship was expected of instrumentalists, but not of singers, and we know that Lowe was a particularly unmusical singer, so that he would have needed Storace's help.

It is surprising to read that a Guard had been engaged to escort patrons from Paddington, then a very sparsely inhabited village which only boasted 341 houses twenty years later. Defoe and Evelyn ignored its existence, and so did their successors, Johnson, Boswell and Walpole. For some reason Messrs. Lowe and Storace decided to woo the inhabitants of this small village, but as far as I know they did not repeat the experiment. Many years later, of course, it was well known as the country home of Sarah Siddons.

For his first season Lowe recruited some talented singers, notably Miss Catley, Miss Plenius, Miss Smith, Miss Froud, Miss Hyat and Mr. Squibb.

The most distinguished of these was Ann Catley. She cannot have been more than 20 when she appeared at Marybone, but her career had started at the age of 10, singing in public houses in the neighbourhood of Tower Hill where she was born. She was apprenticed to William Bates, which ensured a good technical foundation. In 1762 she sang at Vauxhall, and then at Covent Garden in a version of *Comus*. Her subsequent career was on the whole professionally successful, and she was renowned for her lively charm. Rather surprisingly, she married a Colonel Lascelles, by whom she had eight children, and died at the comparatively early age of 40.

Miss Smith and Miss Miles were described as two young Gentlewomen who had never yet sung in public. A note in the Marylebone Collection says that Miss Smith married Charles John Frederick Lampe on 14 May 1763 and was subsequently known as Mrs. Lampe Junior to distinguish her from her mother-in-law, who was still singing in public. J. F. Lampe's 'Six English songs, as sung by Mr. Lowe and

Mrs. Lampe Junior at Marybone Gardens' were published in 1764. Miss Miles, Miss Moyse and Miss Hyat were well known at Marybone at this time.

Miss Catley, Miss Smith, Miss Miles and Thomas Lowe himself sang 'A New Musical Address to the Town' to open the season on 9 May:

> Now the Summer advances and Pleasure removes
>> From the Smoak of the Town to the Fields and the Groves
> Permit me to hope that your Favours again
>> May smile as before on this once happy Plain

sang Lowe to a simple tune which even he could have learnt quite easily (Burney, who admired his voice, said he had to learn most things by ear).

Ann Catley then apologised for Marybone's lack of a Rotunda or a Canal, which were famous features at Rane-lagh:

> Though here no Rotunda expands its wide Dome
> No Canal on its Borders invites ye to roam
> Yet Nature some Blessings has scattered around
> And means to improve may hereafter be found.

A musical promise was then made by the quartet:

> Good Music, Good Wine with each other shall vie.

This promise seems to have been kept. The music may have included some light-weight offerings such as the above, but in those days there was less distinction drawn between 'light' and 'classical', and there was plenty of 'classical', as we should call Arne, Boyce and Handel. As for the wine, it must have been easily obtainable from the adjacent Rose.

The 'New Musical Address' was considered important enough to be printed in the *Gentleman's Magazine*. On its first night it was followed by 'several favourite Songs', the whole to conclude with an Ode, *May Day, or the Shepherd's*

Wedding, first violin Signor Soderigo (?Roderigo), the concert to begin punctually at 6.0 and a 'proper Guard' to be provided to see the Company to and from the Gardens.

On 11 June Handel's *Coronation Anthem* was sung in honour of His Majesty's Birthday, with extra chorus singers engaged from the opera, and a special Guard to conduct patrons from the Gardens as far as the Foundling Hospital, setting off at 10.0, 11.0 and 12.0. This shows how many patrons now came from the Bloomsbury region.

On 28 June there was yet more Handel: *Alexander's Feast*. Handel himself sometimes walked in the Gardens with his friend the schoolmaster, Dr. John Fountain from the Old Manor House. A familiar and possibly apocryphal story has Handel saying to his friend: 'Let us sit down, and listen to this piece' as they strolled by the orchestra. 'I want your opinion of it.' After a while the reverend gentleman said: 'It's not worth listening to – it is very poor stuff.' 'You are right,' replied Handel. 'I thought so myself when I had finished it.'[3]

On 12 August Storace had 'his Night' (i.e. Benefit). There were two solo clarinets, two solo horns and a solo hautboy, as well as the usual strings. The Coronation Anthem was again performed, this time in honour of the Prince of Wales's birthday, also Samuel Arnold's *The Haymakers*, the first of his works to be performed at Marybone, by Miss Smith, Miss Catley, Miss Plenius (another newcomer) and Lowe himself. The evening concluded with 'The Apprentice's Song' sung by Brother Lowe, who was a Freemason.

II

1764

Mrs. Vincent with her 'simple grace'; other singers;
Mr. Squibb is dismissed but returns; Highwaymen
still a menace

The season opened on 9 May 1764, and George Berg seems
to have been the chief composer. On 6 June his 'Ode' was
sung in honour of His Majesty's Birthday, and he wrote songs
specially for Miss Davis and Mr. Lowe.

The singers were much as in 1763, with the important addition of Mrs. Vincent, née Isabella Burchell. She was said
to have been a milkmaid on Jonathan Tyers' country estate.
He gave her a musical training and subsequently 'brought
her out' at Vauxhall, where she was one of the most popular
singers. A sweet natural voice and an unsophisticated style
seem to have been her chief assets. Garrick coached her
as Polly Peachum and she appeared at Drury Lane in 1760
in *The Beggar's Opera* opposite Thomas Lowe, in rivalry
to Charlotte Brent, Arne's 'showy' pupil, and John Beard
at Covent Garden. Charlotte Brent excelled in the bravura;
Isabella Vincent (she married Richard Vincent, the oboe
player, in about 1759) revived the artlessness of Gay's original Polly:

> Lo! Vincent comes with simple grace array'd
> She laughs at paltry arts and scorns parade
> Nature through her is by reflection shown
> While Gay once more knows Polly for his own.

Other and less important additions to the vocal strength

were Miss Davis, Mr. Legg, Mr. Raworth and Mr. Taylor. Mr. Taylor, 'late of His Majesty's Chapel Royal', set a favourite song about a young lady called Maria to be sung by Miss Moyse:

> Is she like the nymphs that still
> Warble on Parnassus' hill
> Or the naiades of the floods,
> Or the draiades of the woods?

Mr. Squibb, who had a Benefit on 19 June, should have included tea and coffee in the evening's entertainment, but this proved 'inconvenient'. There was also some misunderstanding about a ball which had been announced. Whether on account of these contretemps or some other trouble, Mr. Squibb was dismissed during the 1764 season. But he seems to have been forgiven, for he turns up in 1765 again, singing 'Delia' by Jackson of Exeter.

Not satisfied with providing bodyguards for the protection of visitors to the Gardens, Mr. Lowe offered a reward of £10 for the apprehension of any Highwayman found on the road to the Gardens.

Lowe informed 'all decent well behaved people' that they might have the Liberty of walking in the Gardens in the week. Tea and coffee could be had at eight pence per Head, and a Dinner by giving proper Notice.

At the the end of the 1764 season Lowe thanked the Nobility, Gentry and the Rest of his Friends for having generously supported 'the Elegance of Marybone Gardens' during the summer season, and promised 'to merit their future Favour'.

III

1765

*A Fit of the Vapours cured at Marybone; Royal
Occasions; Lowe's financial losses; Building in
Marylebone; Cricket*

The singers for 1765 included Mr. and Mrs. Taylor, Mrs.
Collet, Miss Davis, Mrs. Vincent, Mr. Squibb and of course
Lowe himself. George Berg's 'Ode' and 'Pastoral Dialogue',
and Dr. Boyce's 'Solomon' were among the musical offerings,
also an 'Ode' written and composed by 'A Person of Distinction', and entitled 'The Soldier'.

A 'Puff' in the *Public Advertiser* of 25 August gives a possibly flattering picture of the Gardens this summer. The
writer's 'Fit of the Vapours' was cured when he wandered
into Marybone Gardens and heard the sound of the kettle
drum joined to 'the grand Solemnity of the Organ'; by the
time Thomas Lowe had finished his first song 'the vapourish
Fit' had been turned into a 'Sensation of delightful Extacy'.
Mrs. Vincent's performance of 'Let us wander not unseen'
accompanied by the tintinnabula, an instrument recently
invented by a Mr. Holloway, gave 'exquisite Pleasure'.

Even the refreshments were mentioned and praised for
their moderate cost, and the writer concluded with thanks
to Mr. Lowe for 'the Pains he takes to render his Gardens
worthy the encouragement of the Public'.

On 12 September the *Public Advertiser* published the
words of a 'Semi Chorus from Handel', in which Mrs. Vincent, Miss Davis, Mr. Lowe and Mr. Taylor welcomed to
our shores the Prince and Princess of Brunswick:

64

> Welcome, welcome Royal Pair
> Frederick and Augusta Fair
> Welcome to this Land again
> Free from warlike Toil and Pain.

The Princess had been Princess Augusta of Great Britain, and the Prince had recently covered himself with glory as commander of the Allied Forces at the Battle of Minden.

Another Royal occasion was George III's birthday, celebrated in song by Mrs. Vincent:

> To greet the young Monarch of Britain's blest Isle
> The Groves with gay Blossoms are graced
> The Lily peers forth with an innocent Smile
> And the Roses crowd forward in Haste.

The last two lines conjure up a picture of very strange horticultural phenomena. Poet and composer are alike unknown.

'To oblige the Public', and presumably to give the less musical some suitable entertainment, a Giant, a Dwarf 'and some of their Friends' had taken a Room where they might be seen every evening till the end of the season.

Towards the end of the season Mr. Lowe admitted that he had lost 'upwards of two thousand pounds in the course of the last three seasons' (i.e. 1763, 1764 and the current season, 1765). He appealed to the public and to his friends in particular to support a concert of 'Songs, Catches and Glees' by Purcell and other eminent Masters, also an 'Ode on Masonry'. The Catches and Glees were to be sung by 'three Gentlemen', who would be 'in proper habits' and 'in Character'. In addition, Mr. Clanfield would exhibit 'an elegant Firework' on an entirely new construction, with 'an illuminated Steeple forty Feet high'.

In spite of his own financial troubles Lowe gave the proceeds of an entertainment on 2 October to the sufferers of the late dreadful fires in Montreal in Canada and at Honiton in Devon.

By now, building in Marylebone on both the Portman and

Portland Estates was greatly on the increase, and would eventually threaten the survival of the Gardens. A gentleman returning from Mrs. Vincent's 1764 Benefit remarked that his coach travelled through half a mile of streets in the process of building. He said that Marylebone was a popular residential area, because 'the land Tax' was only two pence in the pound, whereas 'in London' it was five shillings.

But there was still open ground in Marylebone, and at the end of the 1765 season a cricket match was held in Camplings Ground, close by the Church. Cricket and Marylebone were to become synonymous, although the Marylebone Cricket Club would not be founded until 1787, and then on the site of the present Dorset Square, some distance from the 'village'.

IV
1766–1768

Lowe's Bankruptcy; Tokens; 'Young Bloods'; A new route for coaches; A wet season

Lowe had continued to lose money, and on 15 January 1766 his lease (which had eleven years to run) passed into the hands of Messrs. Joseph Beaumont and John Troughton, solicitors, 'on the part of themselves and other creditors'. Beaumont and Troughton had expended of their 'own proper Monies' £263.10.5, and on 28 December John Blandford was paid £1.1.0, 'for keeping possession of Thomas Lowe's Goods, two Days'[4]. The Gardens opened on 1 May.

Lowe continued to sing and to manage the Gardens, the other singers being Mrs. Vincent, Miss Davis, Mr. Taylor and Mr. Raworth. Mr. Collet junior led the orchestra, and Mr. Snow junior played the organ; Seipts and Rathyen, horn-players, and Messrs. Frickler and Hennis, clarinettists, also played 'Choice Pieces'.

The subscription was to be £1.11.6d for two persons, for which a charming little token of mixed metal was issued; 'Admit Two' is surrounded by a formal wreath of acanthus, in which are incorporated two French horns and an open music book (plate 16).

The Tokens were to be obtained from Bremner's Music Shop opposite Somerset House, or of Mr. Eastgate, Hatter and Hosier, of Russell Street, showing that the Managers hoped to draw their clientèle from far afield. But in fact it seems that many Tokens were taken by local tradesmen 'for the accommodation' of their friends and customers.

It was announced that the Company could be accommodated with Tea at eighteenpence a head, but nothing was said about any cakes to accompany the tea.

One Saturday night in 1766 'some young Bloods' took out the pegs which supported the outdoor dancing platform, and immediately 'on the Company's beginning to dance' it gave way, and 'all came down together to the no small Diversion of the Company'. Fortunately no one was hurt.

There was a new 'Coach Way' from Bond Street which avoided the notoriously dirty track by Nibbs Pound where wheels were known to sink five feet down, not an enviable contretemps if you were in your best clothes and on your way to an evening's entertainment. Emerging from Broad Street (Bond Street) you crossed the Oxford Road and passed Oxford Chapel (St. Peter's, Vere Street, built in 1724 by James Gibb), going up Welbeck Street into Marylebone Town (the High Street) and the Gardens. Those who lived in Soho and parts adjacent might come down Portland Street. Thomas Lowe, the Storace family and Ann Catley lived locally, but Mrs. Vincent lodged at More the Grocer's next to the Savoy Gate in the Strand, which gave her a long journey to and from her concerts.

As if to demonstrate that the new route made the journey to and from St. James's possible there is an appeal in one of the 'public prints', dated 15 July 1766, and addressed:

To the Hackney Coachmen and Others

Left in a Hackney Coach coming from Marybone Gardens last night, a small gold horizontal Watch, name Grignion, Number 1590, with an enamelled Dial-plate without Minutes, capped and jewelled, had in it a French-made gold Chain, with a Cornelian Seal set in Gold, Impression a Cypher 'B.B.', a Gold-enamelled heart and a small Ivory Bodkin.

Whoever will bring it to the Earl of Barrymore's in St. James's Place shall receive Ten Guineas Reward; or if offered to be pawned or sold, stop it and the Party, and give Notice to Sir John Fielding, and you shall receive the same Reward.

It was a wet season. At Mrs. Vincent's Benefit on 2 July, a 'Platform entirely covered in' was laid down on the Great Walk (possibly boards to keep the feet dry, and an awning overhead). Horse Patrols were engaged to protect those friends who intended honouring Mrs. Vincent with their presence. Flunkeys carrying umbrellas would possibly have been more useful. The concert consisted of vocal and instrumental music, including several new songs, and ended with a ball, presumably in the Assembly Room.

Acis and Galatea was performed on 26 September, and apparently the early autumn was fine, since the Gardens did not close until 4 October.

There was more rain in the summer of 1767 but Lowe struggled on, with his colleagues: Mrs. Vincent, Miss Davis and Mr. Taylor, with two newcomers, Messrs. Webb and Gibbons. Together on June evenings they sang, among other things, Dr. Arne's Prize Glee 'Which is the properest night to drink?'. (Thomas Augustine can now be legitimately called *Dr.* Arne, having received his doctorate from the University of Oxford in 1759.) Mr. Taylor played a concerto on the organ, and Mr. Clanfield provided fireworks.

There was little else memorable in 1767. In the following year, 1768, Dr. Arne seems to have been the chief composer, and during the season he launched his pupils, Miss Frederic and Master Brown. Other singers were Miss Davis, Miss Froud, Mr. Taylor and Mr. Phillips. *Capochio and Dorina* by Arne, with Miss Frederic and Master Brown in the chief parts, was given on several occasions, with an addition to the orchestra. Preceded by various solos, this was popular for Benefits. On the occasion of Mr. Phillips' Benefit, it was alleged to be the last time Dr. Arne would allow it to be performed. And for that night only Mr. Hook performed a concerto on the harpsichord, probably the first occasion on which his name occurs. The whole was concluded by a grand firework by Mr. Clanfield.

It was announced that a slight Shower or two would not postpone the performance, but if heavy Rains fell it must necessarily be postponed until further notice. Clearly, some heavy rains did fall, causing great disappointment, and Mr. Lowe announced his intention of having the concert in the Assembly Room.

Songs, Catches and Glees remained popular, and Mr. Lowe announced that he would give a morning rehearsal on 2 September of one of these programmes for the benefit of the 'unhappy Sufferers in the Fleet Prison'. His good intentions were frustrated, however, because he would forfeit his Licence if he opened the Gardens before five o'clock in the evening. 'I am absolutely forbid by Act of Parliament to open my Gardens,' he writes, 'before Five in the Evening upon Penalty of forfeiting my Licence.' The use of the first person singular is interesting; writers differ as to the exact date upon which he was obliged to assign to his creditors the receipts and profits of the Gardens, if any. Concerts were held for his benefit, the last being at the Assembly Room on 10 September, on which occasion the Room would be illuminated with wax Lights. He was possibly determined to hang on to the semblance of ownership.

Accounts for the year 1768 are reproduced in Clinch[5] and also in a typescript in the local history collection by Edward S. Foot. Mr. Lowe was given a weekly allowance of £2.2.0, which suggests he was already the employee of his creditors. The receipts for season tickets and money taken at the doors reached the not inconsiderable sum of £2,085.1.7½d, but there was a deficit of £263.10.3d. Mr. Hook is described as 'Music Master', and received four guineas for the week. Master Brown also received four guineas, but most of the singers had two or three guineas. Among the receipts was the sum of £2.14.6 from Dr. Arne 'for Wine'. Twelve Doorkeepers and two Patrols had £4.3.0 for the week between them, but the Watchman only one shilling. One could go on quoting, but there is only one conclusion: in spite of its charms, Marybone Gardens was losing money, and Lowe could not go on. Yet he was optimistic enough to apply to the Justices of the Peace in October 1768 for a renewal of his Licence for the year 1769[6].

The Schedule of Appointments made at the time of Lowe's failure gives important information about the setting for indoor entertainments[7]. The Assembly Rooms had crimson festooned curtains, a pier glass with rich carved gilt frame with four brass arms, two pairs of small pier glasses, an 'orchestra' (i.e. platform suitable for orchestra and soloists), four walnut dining tables, twelve green Windsor chairs, fourteen benches covered with green baize, and a sideboard covered with red baize. Lighting was provided by glass lustres and some glass sconces, presumably lit with wax candles.

Donowell gives us a picture of the company strolling about and listening to music on a fine evening in the Gardens, and perhaps we can make our own picture of what it was all like when the company was forced indoors.

The crimson curtains and pier glasses would have made a charming setting for eighteenth-century music, and, although the hooped dresses and court suits of the ladies and gentlemen on the platform or in the audience may not have been of the first quality, yet they would have looked splendid reflected in the mirrors. Marybone patrons probably did not run to diamonds, but even paste would have had a fine effect.

There was also a Card Room, which contained a harpsichord by Harris, a Music Stand, coloured prints by Hogarth in black and white frames and a mahogany card table.

Somewhere in the Gardens was the so-called Temple, containing the busts of Shakespeare and Handel, which might have been a useful refuge in a sudden shower of rain. There was also a Garden House containing a bust of Milton, two kettle drums, and 'two other drums'.

71

Thomas Lowe

Notes to Part Three

1   A Deed of Assignment made by Thomas Lowe conveying his property in Marybone Gardens to his creditors at the time of his financial collapse in 1769 refers back to the Indenture of 30 August 1763 made between himself and Robert Long, and is the most detailed description of the Gardens we possess. It is reproduced in George Clinch, *Marylebone and St. Pancras*, London, 1890, and elsewhere. Clinch himself says that it was 'formerly in the possession of the late Samuel Hodginson Esq., who allowed an extract to be made for Thomas Smith's *History of the Parish of St. Marylebone*, and published in that work 1833.' The original is not in the Middlesex Records held by the GLC.

   The Ground Landlords of Marybone Gardens were the Portland Estate, and there appear to be insuperable difficulties in tracing this or any other lease in connection with the Gardens. Therefore this 'Copy' is of great value, even if it leaves many questions unanswered.

2   J. T. Smith, *A Book for a Rainy Day*, 1845.

3   This often repeated story seems to have been recorded for the first time in a letter from Norrison Scatcherd, a grandson of Dr. Fountain, to William Hone, and reproduced by him in his *Yearbook*, 1838, under the date of 23 April.

   A different version appears in J. T. Smith's *Nollekens and his Times*, 1825, in which Dr. Fountain says: 'This is damned stuff,' and Handel replies: 'It may be damned stuff, but it is mine.'

4   Edward Foot, Typescript in the St. Marylebone (Library) Collection.

5   Clinch, *op. cit.*, *supra*.

6   See Appendix on Licences.

7   Clinch, *op. cit.*, *supra*.

Part Four

Arnold and Others
1769–1777

I

1769

Arnold, Pinto, Hook and Shakespeare; Illuminations; Grand Firework

Samuel Arnold, well known composer, was assessed for the Rose in 1768, together with John Berry, this being the last year in which Lowe continued to appear, allegedly for the benefit of his creditors.

He had clearly gone downhill vocally as well as financially. When he left Marybone he went to sing at Finch's Grotto Gardens in South London, and other fairly humble tea gardens; also at Sadlers Wells on at least one occasion. He died in Aldersgate Street on 19 March 1783.

In March 1769 *The London Chronicle* announced that Messrs. Troughton and Pinto had purchased the lease of Marybone Gardens for £755. As we have seen, Troughton was one of the two solicitors into whose hands the bankrupt Lowe's lease had passed on 15 January 1765 (the other being Joseph Beaumont). Pinto was born in Naples about 1714, and came to England as something of a musical prodigy. From the middle of the century he was leader and soloist at the Three Choirs, at Drury Lane and (in 1757) at the King's Theatre. In November 1766 he married, as his second wife, Charlotte Brent, the brilliant pupil (and also mistress) of Dr. Arne.

Mrs. Pinto was of course the leading singer of the 1769 season, other singers being Mrs. Forbes, Mr. Reynolds (or Reynoldson), and the Masters Brown and Herryman, with James Hook as composer and organist, who had been listed

75

as Music Master in 1768.

Hook was about 23 at the time, and had been employed for a year at White Conduit House, a minor Tea Garden not far from the present King's Cross Station. He was Norwich-born and had been given his first music lessons by the cathedral organist, with possibly some additional instruction from Dr. Burney, and was at the beginning of a long Pleasure Gardens career. He was already showing signs of the song-writing talent which blossomed in his Vauxhall period. It is estimated that he composed over 2,000 songs, and it is remarkable how many of these have individuality and charm. He had an amazing gift for turning out catchy and singable tunes, and for setting words to music. Grafted on to his early training in English church music was the influence of J. C. Bach (the English Bach) and his 'galant' style. J. C. Bach may also have been responsible for his comparatively early adoption of the 'new' piano forte. Later, he was much drawn to the music of Haydn.

Hook was a minor composer, but in the best eighteenth-century tradition. His musical craftsmanship paralleled the craftsmanship of the lesser silversmiths, cabinet makers and jewellers of the period. As we might deduce from his music, he was a good natured and quick witted person. His elder son, born during the Marybone period, become a distinguished churchman, and Dean of Worcester. Less surprisingly, the second son, Theodore Hook, was a well known novelist, journalist and playwright at the beginning of the next century.

James Hook's first considerable composition for Marybone was the Serenata *Love and Innocence*, first given for Mrs. Pinto's Benefit on 10 August 1769, with Mrs. Pinto herself, Mrs. Forbes, Mr. Reynoldson and the two boys, Brown and Herryman. It was described as 'the first attempt of a young man', and the singers ('especially Mrs. Pinto') gave entire satisfaction. ('Serenata', incidentally, was used in the eighteenth-century to describe not only a Serenade, but also a vocal cantata or even a kind of ode. Handel called his 1720 *Acis and Galatea* a Serenata.)

This Benefit had been postponed on account 'of a very elegant transparent Temple designed and painted by Signor Bigari of the Opera House', which could not be completed by the original date. When finished and shown it was 'allowed by the best Judges to be one of the first Pieces of that kind of Painting to be seen in the Country'.

Serenata and Transparency were again in the programme of James Hook's own Benefit a week later. There were also concertos by Mr. Hook and Mr. Parke on the organ and the oboe respectively 'between the Acts'. John Parke, then about 24, was one of the foremost oboe players of the age. His younger brother, also an oboe player, wrote entertaining if not very reliable 'Musical Memoirs'[1].

There were additional Illuminations in various parts of the Gardens, as well as Signor Bigari's Temple of Apollo, and 'a Grand Firework in Three Divisions', including 'a large Gothic Arch illuminated with Lances, and a large brilliant Sun of eight Points in the Centre, and two Furioni (*sic*) Wheels changing into Wheatsheaves, to conclude with a Battery of Maroons and a Flight of twelve half-point Rockets'.

Tickets, price half-a-crown each, could be obtained of Mr. Hook himself at 4 Great Queen Street, at Welchers' Music Shop in Gerrard Street, the Star and Garter Tavern in Bond Street, or at the Bar of the Gardens.

This splendid entertainment was apparently favoured by the weather, which had been poor earlier in the season. Mr. Hook thanked his patrons in the press on 19 August:

Animated by their favourable Acceptance of his Endeavours, he would study to become even more worthy of their Favours.

Such sycophancy was a matter of course for eighteenth-century performers and composers. Salaries took Benefits into account, and Benefits were dependent on the favours of the moneyed classes. The first Copyright Act of 1709 gave

composers very limited protection, and they were often glad
to sell their work outright for a lump sum.

Love and Innocence was performed a third time for the
Benefit of Mr. Pinto on 24 August, with the same programme
of 'extras', except that in the course of the firework display
two fruit trees burst into full bloom, instead of wheels turning
into wheatsheaves. An English 'Firemaster', Mr. Clanfield,
was responsible, although Signor Rossi was also on the staff.

It was recorded at the Middlesex Quarter Sessions on 5
October 1769 that Thomas Pinto and Samuel Arnold had
'purchased House and Gardens called Marybone since the
last time of licensing', but Pinto and his wife barely survived
the 1769 season. Arnold was to remain for several years.

Arnold's musical contribution was considerable. He wrote
an Ode for the Prince of Wales's birthday on 14 August,
the words by 'the Rev. Mr. Scott', performed by the usual
singers. The Temple of Apollo was exhibited for the second
time, there was a Grand Firework, and the whole concluded
with a Ball, for which a covered platform had been erected.
This patriotic entertainment was repeated at least four times
during the season.

A 'Musical Entertainment' called *Gli Scherzi delle Muse*
was given for the combined Benefits of Signor Storace, Mr.
Richards and Mr. Piguenit (Treasurer, bookseller of Norris
Street). The 'magnificent Firework' by Mr. Clanfield showed
the attack and defence of a fortress in 'a new Construction'
created under the direction of Signor Storace. This sheds
a new light on his talents. Designing scaffolding for a pyrotechnic display can hardly have been part of the training
of a double-bass player. After a temporary eclipse during
Lowe's last year, perhaps visiting his native Italy, Storace
was once more much in evidence.

Marybone always tried to keep up to date, and one of
London's talking points in the late summer of 1769 was the
belated celebration of Shakespeare's bicentenary, known as
the Shakespeare Jubilee. Garrick's ambitious Jubilee at

Stratford was ruined by bad weather, but he was to compensate for this by putting on the pageant devised for Stratford at Drury Lane in October. It ran for 90 performances. The renewal of interest in Shakespeare's plays was largely due to Garrick's revivals during his 19 years as actor-manager.

It was therefore almost inevitable that Arnold should produce an 'Ode in Honour of Shakespeare', performed on 23 September, just before the end of the season. The words were by Francis Gentleman, who spoke the recitatives, with vocal parts sung by the usual singers, followed by the inevitable Temple of Apollo, fireworks, and illuminations: fancy dresses, but no masks allowed.

Gentleman was a Dublin-born actor who had written various plays, and edited Bell's Acting Edition of Shakespeare. He was a somewhat unattractive character, but his collaboration gave a touch of authenticity to the Marybone Jubilee.

Thomas Pinto, like others connected with Marybone, succumbed to financial pressures, and after the 1769 season fled to Scotland to escape his creditors, taking his wife with him. He played at Edinburgh and Aberdeen, and in 1773 went to Dublin where he was appointed leader of the Smock Alley Orchestra. He died in 1783. His wife sang with little success in Dublin, returned to England after his death and devoted herself to the musical education of her husband's grandson, a talented violinist/singer and composer. The once brilliant Miss Brent outlived her powers, and died in poverty as Mrs. Pinto in 1802.

So much for the rather sad story of the Pintos after their brief success at Marybone Gardens.

II

1770

The Barthelemons*, Samuel Arnold, Thomas Chatterton and more James Hook; Fireworks, elegant or magnificent

The Pintos were succeeded by another husband-and-wife team, Mr. and Mrs. Barthelemon. He was composer and leader of the orchestra, and she principal woman singer. Francis Barthelemon was French-born, and his wife, Mary or Polly Young, was a niece of Mrs. Arne, who had brought her up in the best vocal school, mistress of all the technique required by musical fashion although not as 'showy' a singer as Mrs. Pinto. She had made her début at Covent Garden in 1762, and later sang at the King's Theatre where Barthelemon led the orchestra from 1765–1766. His opera *Pelopida* was performed in 1766, and in the same year he married Polly Young; Burney speaks of his 'powerful hand' and 'truly vocal adagio'.

Mrs. Thompson, described by one writer as the sauciest baggage on the modern stage, was engaged as a foil to the more serious Mrs. Barthelemon, and with Mrs. Thompson the very popular bass, Charles Bannister, who was having an affair with her at the time. Charles Bannister was famed for his magnificent bass voice, his talent for mimicry (in which he used his falsetto), and his reputation as a *bon viveur*. He attributed his vocal stamina to his habit of gargling with port wine.

---

* I have used Barthelemon without accents throughout as it was spelt thus in the eighteenth century.

A second bass was engaged, Frederick Charles Reinhold, already well known at Marybone. He was a 'serious' singer and a good musician, at one time organist of St. George's, Bloomsbury, whereas Charles Bannister was largely self-taught, so that each kept to his own style, and there was probably no ill feeling between them.

A Master Cheney, boy soprano, was also engaged, and Mr. Hook remained organist and composer. Under Arnold's régime the musical side of Marybone was very strong. Master Cheney was billed to sing Chatterton's *The Revenge*; his name at least appears in a printed copy of one of the songs.

There is a mystery about the alleged performance on 6 July of *The Revenge*. The music was by Samuel Arnold to a book by Thomas Chatterton, sold by the poet early in the summer for five guineas to a Mr. Atterbury, who was in some way associated with Samuel Arnold in the management. The date of the performance, projected or actual, '6 July', was on the marble-covered copybook containing the manuscript, and it was published in the poet's *Complete Works* in 1803. Even the singers were listed: Bannister as Bacchus, Reinhold as Jupiter and Master Cheney as Cupid. But an undated note in the Marylebone Library states that it was 'Never acted at Marylebone', and doubt has been cast on the assertion that Arnold had already written the music. Dr. Roger Fiske, however, thinks that it may have been performed, since a song 'Away to the Woodlands' was published as 'Sung by Master Cheney'. There is evidence that Chatterton himself visited the Gardens, and the Burlettas performed there may have given him the idea of producing something similar with Arnold as composer. Chatterton committed suicide on 23 August.[2]

Marylebone now had three 'staff' composers: Samuel Arnold, Barthelemon and James Hook, who between them kept the Burletta Theatre and the concerts well supplied. The inevitable *Serva Padrona* was given with 'additions' by Samuel Arnold – including an extra Act in which Charles

Bannister appeared. Mrs. Thompson was the soubrette heroine.

Another 'arrangement' was a Pasticcio called *The Madman*, with music 'from' Piccini, Vento, Arne, Dibdin, Burney, 'etc.', in which Mrs. Barthelemon, Mrs. Thompson and the two basses, Bannister and Reinhold, sang, with 'Varieties of Imitations' introduced by Bannister. Books of the piece were to be purchased at the Bar of the Gardens only, all others being pirated. This hotchpotch was followed by 'an elegant Firework', after which horns and clarinets performed.

Original work for the little Theatre was provided by Barthelemon in his Burlettas *The Magic Girdle* and *The Noble Pedlar*, in both of which his wife sang the lead. *The Noble Pedlar* was repeated at Drury Lane the following year, and its libretto considered important enough to be advertised in *The Gentleman's Magazine* for August 1770.

Benefits included one or more of these new works, as well as extras and guest performances. Mr. Barthelemon was assisted at his benefit by Mr. Rogers of Bath ('Mr. Leander's Scholar') and Master Green ('Mr. Jones's Scholar'). The Leander Brothers excelled on the French horn, and Mr. Jones was a leading trumpet player. The 'scholars' were probably the equivalent of apprentices, who paid a proportion of their earnings in return for their instruction.

At Mr. Richard's Benefit on 4 September the *Serva Padrona* was performed, and Messrs. Barthelemon and Hook played concerti on the violin and organ respectively. The Fourth Concerto by Corelli had additional parts for trumpets, French horns and kettle drums. There was dancing in the 'Large Room of the House', fireworks, and (even more important) a Full Moon. Either the neighbourhood of Marybone was now less infested with footpads, or Samuel Arnold was careless of his patrons' safety; there seem to have been no more armed escorts. But a Full Moon must have been an asset.

Hook called his Benefit (on 11 September) A Grand Festival, moon or no moon. In the main it was a resumé of the season's successes with some guest performers: Mr. Cohen, 'Musician to the Stadtholder', played a concerto on the French horn – his first appearance in England – and two young ladies sang for the first time in public. The magnificent firework was under the direction of Mr. Clitherow.

III

1771

Burlettas and 'the usual musical Entertainments';
usual Fireworks

In 1771 and 1772 the Barthelemons were absent in Ireland.
Barthelemon's successor as First Violin and Leader of the
Orchestra is not specifically named before the season opened,
but on 27 May 'Mons. Reeves', 'being his first appearance in
public', is 'Solo Violin' and is mentioned several times later
on, and it is a reasonable supposition that as his first appearance was apparently satisfactory he became Leader. Perhaps
for the first night one of the band took on the task. Hook
presumably directed from the keyboard, except for Arnold's
own compositions, which he would have directed himself.

The first night of the season opened with a safe draw:
La Serva Padrona, with Mrs. Thompson, and Messrs. Reinhold and Bannister, and 'New Musical Imitations' by Mr.
Bannister. Except for the additional services of 'A Young
Lady who never sung in Public before', there was nothing
new. Mr. Hook played a concerto on the organ, Mr. Rossi
displayed an elegant Firework, and subscription tickets at
two guineas were obtainable from Mr. Piguenit, bookseller,
of Norris Street, Haymarket (he later moved to Berkeley
Square), Mr. Story, silversmith of Leicester Square, and the
Bar of the Gardens.

The singers were Mrs. Thompson, Miss Thomas, a Miss
Esser who accompanied herself on the violin, Mrs. Cart-
wright, Miss Ann Catley, Miss Harper (who later married
Jack Bannister, a great favourite of Charles Lamb, son of

84

Charles Bannister) and the two basses, Charles Bannister and Reinhold.

The first performance of Arnold's *The Magnet*, text by Lady Dorothy Dubois, was on 27 June, sung by Mrs. Thompson, Miss Thomas and Mr. Bannister – the Burletta team. This was repeated several times, and was a popular choice for Benefits.

Other Burlettas performed by the same team were *A Cure for Dotage* (the composer uncertain) and *The Coquet*, a much altered version of *Il Cicisbeo alla Moda* of 1759. It was translated from the Italian of Goldoni and adapted to the music of Galuppi by 'Signor Storace, Compiler of *La Serva Padrona*'.

Mr. Bannister chose *La Serva Padrona* for his Benefit, and had the additional services of Mrs. Sophia Baddeley in 'Musical Imitations', a beautiful woman and distinguished actress, with a good singing voice, and notorious for her 'dissipation', as it was called.

Ann Catley sang "Sweet Echo' with flute obbligato and 'Water parted from the sea', 'after the manner of the original' for her Benefit in the intervals of *The Magnet*. Ann Catley took no part in the Burlettas, but was clearly regarded as an important soloist as she was given a Benefit to herself.

Reinhold showed his musicianship on at least one occasion by playing a concerto on the organ as well as singing a part in *A Cure for Dotage*.

Mrs. Thompson's Benefit had *The Coquet* as its *pièce de résistance*, and in addition to her part she sang a rousing hunting song, 'With Horn and With Hounds'.

A 'puff' in the press said that Mrs. Thompson and Miss Thomas 'have merit in the burlettas, a species of Entertainment lately come greatly into Vogue in England'. This was somewhat out-of-date, seeing that Burlettas were first introduced at Marybone in 1758.

Most evenings' entertainments, weather permitting, were rounded off by 'an elegant Firework' by Signor Rossi.

IV

1772

Torre and his very unusual Fireworks; Pyrotechnics and classical myths; Garrick encourages him to come to England; Alarming rumours about his career in France; Problems of the Licence; Mrs. Fountain and her fellow-protesters; Torre triumphs; Dr. Johnson's night out

Fireworks, elegant or magnificent, had been a pleasantly spectacular way of rounding off an evening of music, meeting friends, strolling about, and supper. But now they were to become the chief feature of a Marybone evening.

'The Celebrated Signore Torre' had first come to Marybone in 1753, as we have seen, but did not stay long. It is unlikely that he had then developed his special form of entertainment which went far beyond elegant fireworks. During his nineteen years on the Continent he had been studying and experimenting[3].

By the middle of the eighteenth century pyrotechnics had split into the Southern School – Italy, Spain and France – and the Northern School – Germany, Holland and eventually England. Briefly, the Southern School relied mainly on an architectural structure, or 'Machine' as it was called, of considerable size and elaboration; it could be up to 400 feet long, and semi-permanent. In the eighteenth century architecture was considered the first of the arts, and might symbolise the dynastic principle as well as reminding the viewers of the glories of Greece and Rome. From a practical point of view, the architectural features were useful as a means of concealing the fireworks and their operators. The Northern School, on the other hand, relied less on architecture; they spent less money on 'solid' backgrounds, preferring painted backdrops. The fireworks were on show in front of the machine, with their cases tied on ready for firing.

Torre, himself a Southerner – 'Artificer to the Emperor' and 'Chief Engineer to the King of France' – was independent enough to adapt other styles to his needs when it suited him.

Most important, especially for the story of Marybone, he was one of the first, if not the first, to create a semi-theatrical semi-pyrotechnical entertainment, depicting the classical myths so dear to the eighteenth century, using actors to mime the scenes, and every resource of the fireworker's art for the 'effects'. These so-called Exhibitions of Torre were to be the sensation of Marybone in 1772–1774, causing not only astonishment and delight, but also protests and legal battles. Torre's 'Magnificent Fireworks' may or may not have been superior to those of his rivals, but his Exhibitions were in a class apart.

Torre was both artist and scientist. Taught by his friend Réaumur he made barometers, and had a shop in Paris which he called 'Cabinet de Physique experimentale'. 'Physique experimentale' must also have been a vital element in his fireworks[4].

The high point of Torre's French career was his display of fireworks at Versailles in honour of the marriage of the Dauphin and Marie Antoinette in 1770. But sometime thereafter he lost his Licence through a political intrigue. Jean Monnet, former director of the Opéra Comique, wrote to his good friend Garrick in London, pleading the unlucky situation of Torre, 'a great genius'. Garrick's reply was that he should come over to England as soon as possible[5].

Torre travelled to England in the company of Philippe Jacques de Loutherbourg, a scene painter also recommended to Garrick by Jean Monnet. They are likely to have met already in Paris, and must have had a great deal in common.

It is probable that both had studied under Servandoni, the French scenic artist. In his later career in England Loutherbourg was an innovator in various stage effects, and in the production of illusions of sunsets, fire, volcanos and movements of clouds. Torre also worked in light and in illusion. It would be interesting to know if they influenced each other's work. Their friendship certainly continued in England and, when the versatile Torre took to publishing prints instead of exhibiting fireworks, Loutherbourg's *Caricatures of the English* was one of his publications. The scene painter became scenic director to Garrick and later to Sheridan.

Garrick sent Torre with an introduction to the Managers of Ranelagh. They failed to agree terms, although the Managers paid Torre's travelling expenses. Torre then went to Messrs. Arnold and Berry, and they entered into a contract 'for the whole term of Lease of Gardens'; Torre was to erect buildings; and they entered into a Bond for £1,000 'for Observation of the said Contract'[6].

But before Torre signed Garrick was 'desired to attend' to make sure the parties understood one another, which he was satisfied was the case. Garrick seems to have done his very best to see Jean Monnet's friend well established.

Although fireworks had been exhibited in the various public gardens for at least twenty years 'without legality being questioned', Messrs. Arnold and Berry were clearly aware that Torre's 'Exhibitions' were in a class apart. 'Many respectable persons', however, had informed them that provided Torre obtained a Licence from the Board of Ordnance they would be legally covered. Torre obtained the required Licence.

All this must have been done before October, the time when proprietors of Gardens, etc., applied for their 'Musick Licence' for the following year.

Not expecting any objection on general grounds and knowing that Torre had his own Licence from the Board of Ordnance, Arnold was quite unprepared for the terrible shock of being refused the Public Musick Licence for the following year, 1772. All his schemes tumbled about his ears, and he faced being subject to the penalties of non-fulfilment of his bond with Torre, and also answerable to his partner, Berry. Such a refusal was incomprehensible, except in the supposition that Sir John Hawkins at the Middlesex Sessions had heard from France some of the rumours about Torre so soon to circulate, and thought it unwise to let that gentleman loose.

Disaster threatened. Torre, Berry and Arnold faced ruin. Marybone would have lacked the most colourful of its episodes. Fanny Burney's *Evelina* would have missed an important adventure. This chapter would have come to an abrupt end.

Instead of which that ultra-respectable-looking gentleman, Samuel Arnold – soon to be Dr. Samuel Arnold and eventually to find his last resting place in Westminster Abbey – decided to ignore the Justices and their Licence, and continue with his plans, the first of which was to erect 'a very large and handsome Building, elegantly decorated'. Torre also must have had many technical preparations to make, as well as the engaging of dramatic and technical assistants. A machine would have to be constructed and erected.

Some time before the proposed opening (the third week in May 1772):

> . . . a large Cargo of the necessary apparatus for a new and very singular kind of Fireworks arrived from France, and was brought in a train of carts to Marybone Gardens. The extraordinary appearance and declared use of these machines occasioned universal alarm.

These carts lumbering along the rail-and-post boundary which was all that marked off the New Road from the surrounding fields must have seemed sinister visitants from that wicked country, France.

Advance publicity made much of Torre's achievement and royal connections, and the uniqueness of his art. But ugly rumours also circulated: Nine hundred people had been 'blown up' on the occasion of the Dauphin's wedding. This was contradicted, but it was alleged that 132 persons had been crushed to death as they left the fireworks.

A writer to the press warned 'Mr. A and Mr. B.' that if a single life were lost it would be charged to their account.

On 2 June Torre published a long and dignified disclaimer through the medium of *The Gazeteer*. He submitted the following facts:

Although there was an uncommon concourse of people at the Versailles celebrations, no one received the least hurt. Eight days later, the Artificers of the City of Paris put on a display with which Mr. Torre had no connections, and many unhappy people lost their lives through hurrying along a street filled with coaches and horses. A few weeks later the Spanish Ambassador had employed Torre to give a display before forty thousand people, which took place with safety and success.

A personal calumny that he had blown up his own wife and child was easily refuted: his wife was with him in perfect health, and his child was at boarding school.

Besides these accusations against Torre, opposition was also being mobilised upon what we should now call environmental grounds. The opening was postponed from Wednesday, 20 May, until Saturday, 23 May, and turned out to be an anti-climax. The Exhibition had been injured by the damp, before the performance, and had apparently been finished off by a high wind. Disappointment was great. A small audience, however, applauded Mrs. Cartwright, making her début as a singer.

But the local protesters were not to be put off, though they had little to protest about. On Monday, 25 May, residents presented a petition to the Justices at Bow Street requesting them to stop such exhibitions. Much of the following story has been told in various books on Marybone, but incompletely, and omitting many particulars.

Mrs. Fountain (who kept the boarding school for young ladies near the Gardens) said that her pupils retired to rest as usual one evening at nine o'clock when they were awakened and terribly frightened by an explosion. She apprehended danger from falling rockets, etc. Elizabeth Hart, her servant, said she had seen the 'bomb' burst in the air, and Mrs. Fountain produced some burnt paper which she alleged was the remains of the said 'bomb'.

Mr. Russell, a clergyman, deposed that the noise gave much uneasiness to the sick and infirm whom it was his duty to visit, and that if he opened a window his furniture was so covered with dust that he could write upon it with his finger.

And Mr. Thomas Willis, who had gout in the head, said that the noise kept him awake at night, and he had to sleep away from home.

Moreover, the coaches resorting to Marybone were so numerous that people could not get to their own houses. This last complaint, which is one all too familiar in the twentieth century, showed that the fireworks attracted many people living at a distance from Marybone Gardens, and it is clear that Mr. Arnold would not give up such a money-spinner without a struggle.

The first round was won by Mrs. Fountain and her fellow-protesters. The Treasurer of Marybone (Mr. Piguenit) was told the Gardens would lose their Licence unless the fireworks were discontinued. Nobody seems to have known that Marybone did not have a Licence for 1772, anyway.

The proceedings seem to have been hilarious. A 'witticism' of some kind having 'arisen' (*sic*) concerning 'Mons. Torre', Sir John Fielding from the Bench observed that probably a Frenchman would not care if he were to blow up all Marybone, which was a curious remark to make from the Bench. Mrs. Fountain repeated the popular accusation that he had already blown up his own wife and children (in the plural this time). Everyone knew that Torre was a foreigner, but what kind of foreigner was in some doubt.

A letter to the *London Evening Post* praised Mrs. Fountain for her Piety and exemplary Conduct in the matter and asserted that the whole of Marybone was 'offended'. A reply to the same journal scoffed at this estimate of Mrs. Fountain, and said that the 23 signatures had only been obtained by 'cajoling, threatening and deceit'. Many of these persons recanted and 'deserted the Schoolmistress', and at the adjourned hearing 40 people appeared in favour of Torre.

On 2 July Mr. Arnold, as proprietor of Marybone Gardens, was summoned to Bow Street to pay a fine of £5 for 'causing Fireworks to be made contrary to the Act of 9th and 10th of William III'. The Act provided for two separate offences: one making or causing fireworks to be made, and the other 'throwing or casting fireworks from any house, garden, &c.'. In spite of the deposition of a witness that he had seen 'preparations for fireworks making in the Garden', Mr. Morris (Arnold's Counsel) considered that this verbal evidence was unacceptable. Mrs. Fountain and another lady had produced 'written evidence' in the shape of letters 'as from Mr. Arnold', but they had not even proved his handwriting. Mr. Morris further observed that it was absurd to accuse Mr. Arnold of wishing to annoy the public by whose bounty he lived. It was the opinion of the Bench that Mr. Arnold was not fineable, and the matter seems to have been dropped, in spite of suggestions for an action to be brought at common law for nuisance. To clinch the matter, Mr. Arnold produced the Licence from the Board of Ordnance.

Mrs. Fountain's allegations about Torre's having blown up his wife and children show her as a somewhat hysterical woman, at the least, and there is a hint of attempted forgery in the account of the Arnold letters of which she had not proved the handwriting.

Somewhere about the time of the Bow Street episode an undated cutting in the Marylebone Library describes how 'a very notable schoolmistress (ashamed to be seen at Mary-

bone Gardens)', was at the Sadlers Wells pantomime with
her pretty daughter when some crackers were let off 'deliberately to annoy her', as her 'long aversion and steady opposition to fireworks' was well known. An ironical allusion to
her 'sweet disposition' makes it clear that by this time she
was a notorious figure.

We know that in earlier years she had helped her husband
with his school (see p. 38) but it seems that she was always
an unaccountable person, possibly a real eccentric, in spite
of her reputed kindness to small boys. As years went by
she certainly offended her husband, who spoke of her as
'my most wicked and abandoned wife' and accused her of
squandering his money.

Was this why she left her husband and his pupils, and
established a girls' school next door? An enigmatic, but certainly colourful character.

One of the people most upset by the Bow Street publicity
was David Garrick. Sir John Fielding had told Garrick's
brother that he was surprised that he, David Garrick, should
have countenanced Torre in an illegal act. This may have
been in jest but, as the relations between the two were never
very pleasant, it is more likely that Fielding was deliberately
malicious. At all events, Garrick was touched on the raw,
and defended himself:

All he had done was to recommend an ingenious, worthy
Stranger, recommended by a friend who had been particularly
civil and friendly, Jean Monnet[7].

This presumably blew over, as did the threatened litiga-
tion. After a bad start, Torre's 'Exhibitions' and his fireworks
proved as sensational an attraction as had been hoped.

It is unfortunate that we have verbal descriptions only of
these entertainments. Signor Torre's own scenarios, if one
may so describe them, were certainly detailed and colourful
(see plate 9).

There is a good description of 'his new and uncommon

manoeuvres in fire' in an undated cutting describing the King's Birthday of the year 1772. A 'numerous Appearance of genteel Company' had assembled at Marybone. The first part of the entertainment consisted in various Transparencies of Their Majesties, and a straightforward display of fireworks (suns, wheels, stars, etc.).

Then the curtain rose on the inside of Mount Etna. The raising of the curtain is mentioned more than once, thus emphasising the theatrical nature of the Exhibition. The audience were kept at least 20, sometimes 60, yards away. The action was a kind of masque.

Vulcan led the Cyclops, who lit a fire and forged arrows for Cupid and his mother Venus. The mountain appeared to be on fire, and the lava flowed in a continuous stream, concluding a scene 'uncommonly grand and pleasing'.

Among the genteel Company, however, were some 'City Smarts' who did not understand what was going on, 'for want of a better acquaintance with heathen Mythology'. In other words, they lacked that classical education almost indispensable to the understanding of any form of art in the eighteenth century.

Mr. Ron Harris has given an invaluable description of how effects such as Vulcan's Forge and the volcano were produced by a mixture of rockets fitted to ropes, giving an effect of fire which moved across the arena; with transparent troughs of water lit from below with fire to produce the flow of lava as each segment was revealed.

Dr. Johnson's curiosity was aroused by the Torre publicity, and he decided to go and see the wonders for himself. Unfortunately, he went to Marybone, accompanied by a friend, on a damp night, when 'the Proprietors' announced that the exhibition could not take place. Dr. Johnson thought this a mere excuse, and incited the bystanders to smash the lamps round the Orchestra with their sticks. An attempt was then made to light fireworks, but to no avail; the Proprietors were justified in their refusal to proceed with the show. The story is little to the credit of Dr. Johnson. Presumably he went again on a more favourable night, for he compared the poet Gray with Torre, 'who played his corruscations so speciously that his steel dust is mistaken by many for a shower of gold'. Clearly, he had seen fireworks only, not a dramatic exhibition[8].

V

1772

Music in the early days of Torre; James Hook and
the Piano Forte; Thomas Linley the Younger

Torre and his works did not entirely overshadow the music.
Concerts and burlettas continued, with Arnold, Hook and
Storace much in evidence. Mrs. Forbes, Mrs. Cartwright,
Miss Wilde and of course Mrs. Thompson were the chief
ladies, with Messrs. Phillips, Culver, Bannister and Reinhold
the chief gentlemen in 1772. Admittedly, Benefits generally
had the additional attraction of one of Torre's set pieces,
advertised in larger print than the music. There were other
'Fireworkers' also, such as Signor Padraio, 'just arrived from
Italy', who exhibited 'a most beautiful Firework' for the benefit of the Doorkeepers, and the Englishmen, Messrs. Clitherow and Clanfield.

Hook's *The Divorce* was a novelty that season with the
four characters represented by Mrs. Forbes, Mrs. Cartwright
and Messrs. Reinhold and Bannister. *The Coquet* was
revived, and of course *La Serva Padrona*.

On the occasion of Mr. Hook's Annual Festival (as he
called his Benefit) on 28 August, *Il Dilettante* by Mr. Hook
himself was given for the first time by Mrs. Thompson, Mr.
Reinhold and Mr. Bannister, with imitations of the German
and Italian styles of singing. It was preceded by an Ode written by Mr. Hook for the opening of the new Exhibition Room
of the Royal Incorporated Artists of Great Britain, performed by an augmented Band and Chorus, reinforced by
young Gentlemen from St. Paul's Cathedral choir, with solos

by the Marybone singers; certainly an unusual prelude to a Marybone evening.

Still more unexpected 'for that Night only and by particular Desire', Mr. Hook performed a concerto on the Piano Forte between the Acts of the burletta. This seems to be the first time he played upon this comparatively novel instrument in the Gardens; its first performance in public in London seems to have been in 1768. What make was his Piano Forte, did he keep it at home at his house at 18 Newman Street, and bring it to Marybone 'for this night only' in a coach? What concerto did he play? The third question is easy to answer: instrumentalists usually played show pieces of their own composition on such occasions. But the first two questions, more practical, remain unanswered.

The contrasting musical offerings – Ode, Burletta and Piano Forte Concerto – were followed by an even more surprising item in Signor Torre's magnificent fireworks: a Representation of some Part of Cox's Museum. This was a collection of mechanical models formed by James Cox, exhibited in Spring Gardens, and afterwards dispersed by lottery. At least two exhibits – a moving swan made of silver, and a Perpetual Clock – can still be seen: the first at the Bowes Museum, Barnard Castle, and the second at the Victoria and Albert. How Torre represented this sort of thing in fireworks or even in transparencies is hard to imagine[9]. Besides this Representation, he exhibited a variety of more conventional fireworks, and also a 'Most Magnificent Temple', 'new for the night', with a musical accompaniment of martial music, also 'new for the night', composed by Mr. Hook, instrument or instruments not stated.

An important guest artist boosted Storace's Benefit on 31 August: Thomas Linley the younger, son of Thomas Linley of Bath. He was born in the same year as Mozart, and they studied violin together at Florence under Nardini when they were both fourteen. They became friends and shed tears at parting. Back in England, young Linley led his father's Bath orchestra, and was a soloist at Drury Lane and elsewhere. He also helped his father in some compositions, and had some songs and theatre music to his own credit. When he played at the Storace Benefit he was 16; six years later he was drowned in a boating accident.

A revival of *The Coquet* was the main piece of the evening, but it has to be admitted that Signore Torre's name appeared in larger print than that of any of the musicians. His Grand Exhibition was to conclude the evening, but on this occasion he did not commit himself to any particular programme, since his

> Reputation being so well known makes it unnecessary to particularise any Pieces he will exhibit; he chuses rather to surprise than fall short of the public Expectation; and flatters himself, his Exhibition that Night will give general Satisfaction, as his Views are rather Glory than Profit.

The 'Views' of the musicians who relied so much on their Benefits to make a living may not have been so high-minded as those that Torre claimed for himself.

As Torre had brought such fame to Marybone, it seemed only fair that he should be allotted two Benefits, instead of the usual one. At one of these he showed Hercules delivering Theseus from Hell, instead of the advertised Forge of Vulcan, claiming that 'the Introduction of every Character and Circumstance and whatever is proper to the Subject cannot fail of rendering it an interesting Spectacle'. He assured the public that nothing would be neglected to convince them of his fervent desire to please. Pyrotechnists had to be as sycophantic as musicians.

VI

1773

Torre's triumphs continued; Return of the Barthelemons; Charles Dibdin; Dr. Burney and his daughter; Evelina sees Torre's 'Orpheus and Euridice' and has an adventure; A Moral Tale

The Barthelemons returned in time for the opening of the 1773 season. The Gardens were open three times a week only: Monday, Wednesday and Friday. A subscription valid for one evening a week cost three guineas for two persons. The entertainments would exceed in 'Novelty, Variety and Elegance', anything previously given at Marybone. Additional illuminations and some exceedingly beautiful transparencies would be displayed, and on the fourth night of the subscription 'a magnificent Firework'. This was certainly to be one of Marybone's most exciting seasons, yet Arnold had again been refused a Licence.

Early in the season Handel's *Acis and Galatea* was given 'in a new Manner and with great Judgement'. What was this new manner? Something like a dramatic concert? Mrs. Barthelemon was the Galatea, Mrs. Thompson the Acis, Mr. Reinhold the Polytheme, and Miss Wilde the Floris, 'receiving just encouragement for the first of many performances that season'. *Acis* was repeated several times, and in June was preceded by 'A Comic Act by the Three Italian Musicians blind from their Birth', and a concerto on the violin by Mr. Barthelemon.

An important newcomer was 'Mr. Dibdin of Drury Lane'. He was born in 1745, and had already a considerable reputation as singer, actor, composer and adapter. The sea songs for which he is most famous were yet to come, but he had already written several musical pieces for Covent Garden and Drury Lane, notably *The Padlock* in which he sang Mungo.

Bannister was no longer on the roster of singers. The ladies were Mrs. Barthelemon, Miss Wilde and Mrs. Thompson, and the gentlemen Mr. Phillips, Mr. Reinhold and Charles Dibdin.

Besides *Acis and Galatea*, other musical entertainments were revivals, with two new pieces by Arnold, *La Zingara or the Gipsies* and *The Wedding Day*. *La Zingara* was given for Mr. Barthelemon's Benefit on 25 August, with Mrs. Barthelemon, Dibdin and Phillips. It was preceded by 'A Variety of Vocal and Instrumental Music', including a violin concerto by Barthelemon himself in which 'A Favourite Irish Air' was introduced, probably a reminiscence of his stay in Dublin. Mr. Hook played a concerto on the organ, Master Archer, 'Mr. Barthelemon's Scholar', played a solo on the trumpet, surely an unusual instrument for a violinist's pupil to choose.

On this occasion the final fireworks were supplied not by Signor Torre, but by Monsieur Caillot (Fireworker to Ranelagh). He exhibited 'Capital Transparencies' called 'The Destruction of the Macaronies', followed by a firework display, but this entertainment was not in the Torre line. Possibly weather conditions had made it essential to have something less demanding in reserve.

Hook's 'Grand Festival' was included two nights later, and his *Apollo and Daphne* and *The Divorce*, a violin concerto by Mr. Barthelemon and a Piano Forte Concerto by Hook, which he performed himself, with variations on 'Lovely Nancy'.

Then came Signor Torre's 'Exhibition Extraordinary' which included 'Les Galeries de Florence', followed by *Orpheus and Euridice*, after which the Gardens were illumi-

nated in a singular and elegant manner. Tickets price 3s. 6d.
were obtainable from Mr. Hook himself (now in Richmond
Buildings; he seems to have moved fairly often) and various
familiar places such as Welcker's and Slaughter's.

Torre was never satisfied with his achievements. The fire
after *Orpheus and Euridice* was held to be as magnificent
as possible, yet he promised to make 'a most surprizing addition' to that admirable performance, which seems to have
been particularly splendid. According to an undated cutting,
there were several scenes where the flitting to and fro of
the spirits was clearly rendered by means of transparent
gauze, interposed between the actors and the spectators.

Torre made an excursion into Chinoiserie during the 1773
season:

A Representation of the Election of the Emperor of China, with
the Introduction of every Character, Circumstance and whatever
is proper to their various Performances, cannot fail rendering
them elegant and surprizing; they will be proceeded [*sic*] by an
Intermixture of all Kinds of Fire, too tedious to particularize.
The Dresses and Decorations entirely new.

Torre gave this for his own Benefit on 9 July; it had been
fixed for the previous Friday when wet weather exceedingly
damaged his Firework, and the Managers therefore 'gave
him another Opportunity to display his Exhibition in its full
Splendour'. Among the addresses given for tickets was that
of 'Mr. A. Torre, The Golden Head, Market Lane behind
the Opera House'; this must have been his son Antony who
later played an important part in the history of Colnaghi.

It would be interesting to know how Torre or some assistant 'directed' the actors in the Exhibitions. The spirits who
flitted to and fro were probably dancers, as were possibly
some of the other actors, as their parts were mimed. In the
summer season out-of-work dancers or actors would not have
been difficult to find. But someone – the versatile Torre himself? – must have trained them to act their parts among

exploding fireworks; someone must have 'directed' the dramatic side. One suspects that costumes might have been borrowed 'second hand' from one of the theatres, in spite of the assurance that in 'The Emperor of China' they were entirely new.

Torre must have had a considerable staff behind the scenes. Clearly he was the inspirer and designer of these Exhibitions, but they could not have gone off so smoothly without an efficient back-up.

On the technical side alone he must have relied upon many humble 'Artists, Artificers and Mechanics', and it is good to know that he provided them with a Benefit that season, a concert of horns and clarinets.

Rather late in the season, 6 September, what was called an AMBARVALIA was held, with Reinhold as Bacchus and Phillips as Principal Arval Brother, Mrs. Barthelemon as Ceres, and a chorus. The Ambarvalia was preceded by a concert of vocal and instrumental music by the usual performers, and followed by a Magnificent Firework 'suitable to the Occasion', with Decorations and Emblematical Transparencies'. The whole was to conclude with a 'A GRAND CEREALIA'. The Gardens would be illuminated in a new style suitable to the Ambarvalia. This description is somewhat vague, as if the organisers were not quite sure what an Ambarvalia meant.

For one night only, 15 September, Bonnell Thornton's Burlesque Ode, with music by Dr. Burney, was performed by various artists using burlesque names, preceded by Glees conducted by Dr. Arne. This curious entertainment was also given at Ranelagh. Torre promised Fireworks 'in a comic Stile', being an attempt entirely new. Humour is something one does not associate with Torre, and it does not seem as if he tried it again.

Dr. Burney himself had taken a party to Marybone in June of the same year, consisting of his daughters Susan and Fanny and Mr. and Mrs. Young. At that time the Burneys were living at the upper (northern) end of Queen's Square, which had a beautiful view across fields to Hampstead and Highgate, and was therefore within fairly easy reach of Marybone Gardens. As mentioned earlier, Dr. Burney was a great admirer of Mr. Barthelemon's playing.

Fanny chose to send her heroine, Evelina, to Marybone Gardens at about the same period, although the novel *Evelina* was not published until 1778, by which time the Gardens had disappeared. Evelina was staying in Holborn, not a very aristocratic neighbourhood, with the vulgar Branghton family who took her to the Gardens. Young Branghton attached himself to Evelina and suggested: 'Come, Miss, let you and I have a little fun together . . .' Evelina did not care for that sort of 'fun'. More to her taste was a concerto on the violin by Mr. Barthelemon, 'a player of exquisite taste and fancy'.

When it was time for the fireworks the whole party hurried to get good seats, and found *Orpheus and Euridice* really beautiful. But at the moment of the 'fatal look' there was an explosion, perhaps similar to that which had so frightened Mrs. Fountain's young ladies. Evelina and her companions were so startled that they all scattered in different directions, and she was separated from her party. Various encounters with undesirable characters further frightened the timorous and circumspect Evelina, but at last they were all reunited.

Something much more distressing then occurred: they met Lord Orville. This simple statement does not do justice to the emotions aroused in the bosoms of the chief characters. *He* was surprised to see her in such company, and *she* was ashamed to admit that she was staying with the Branghtons in Holborn . . . *Holborn*! Lord Orville lived in Berkeley Square. In spite of this setback, however, two hundred or so pages later Evelina married Lord Orville.

A lesser known heroine of eighteenth-century fiction, Eliza of 'The Marybone Evening', published in a periodical 'for Ladies', also visited the Gardens in the early 1770s.

Eliza, the fair daughter of a prosperous tradesman who lived in Snow Hill, Holborn, was courted by Jack, the worthless son of a country gentleman. Jack's intentions were far from honourable, since he thought himself superior to a family 'in trade', but he convinced everyone, including Eliza, that he planned to marry her, so successfully that she became increasingly 'free' in her deportment when in his company, which encouraged him in his evil designs. The author does not specify in what this 'freedom' of deportment consisted, which is somewhat disappointing.

One evening Jack suggested a little party to Marybone, as a new Burletta was to be performed by Mrs. Thompson and Mr. Bannister. It was to be a foursome: Jack and Eliza, with Charles (his friend) and Nancy (Eliza's friend). Parental permission was obtained, and they set forth in a coach. Nancy was 'vastly fond' of Marybone, considering it 'an excessive genteel Place'. The music fully answered their expectations, but while they were watching the fireworks Eliza began to be concerned for her parents, for some curious reason, and wished to go home. Jack went to look for their coach, but returned in mock dismay with the information that their coachman had 'gone off'. The anxious Eliza suggested walking home, but Jack met a lady and her daughter, supposed friends of his, who offered places in their own coach. Off they went, but the coach turned down south towards Cavendish Square, instead of east to Holborn, the direction of Snow Hill. Eliza suddenly felt faint, and had to be carried into a house, supposedly that of Jack's friend, Mrs. Oswald. This lady put her to bed, and Jack promised to take a letter to her parents. Needless to say, he did nothing of the sort, but proceeded to take advantage of her weakness. She had unfortunately given him some unspecified encouragement, albeit innocently, and now she was overcome by his 'superior rhetoric and elocution', as the writer put it.

The same fate might have befallen Nancy, but she was more alert and threatened Charles with a penknife.

Next morning the two girls found themselves a hackney coach, and returned to Snow Hill, Eliza overcome with tears and remorse, and Nancy probably rather smug.

The end of the story was perhaps happier than anyone deserved. Although he had had no intention of marrying a tradesman's daughter, Jack's father insisted on his doing so. He had doubtless ascertained that the tradesman was prosperous. Their marriage was celebrated in the presence of both sets of parents. Jack made an exemplary husband, and Eliza the most deserving of wives.

This cautionary tale displays in a cruder form the same class consciousness as does *Evelina*. It was difficult to step across the boundaries of degree in the eighteenth century. Between Berkeley Square and Holborn a great gulf was fixed, which money of course could help to bridge. Fanny Burney herself was as conscious as anyone of social nuances. She was not connected with trade, and her father was a highly respected scholar, but he was a professional musician, and her appointment as Keeper of the Robes to Queen Charlotte was a social advance, although a kind of servitude.

In the second story it is taken for granted that, although Jack was originally described as 'worthless' and had unscrupulously taken advantage of a girl who was his social inferior, yet marriage made everything right, and of course Eliza took a step up in the world. The author was in a moral dilemma, and was careful to condemn 'free' behaviour such as Eliza's, in spite of the happy ending.

A laconic statement appeared in the press some time during that same year, 1773, which reminds us of yet another aspect of eighteenth-century life taken for granted then but shocking to twentieth-century minds:

> Two young Men were hanged at Tyburn for robbing the Marybone Waiters.

VII

1774

Discovery of a Mineral Spring; Burlettas and concerts; Lecture on Shakespeare; Farewell to Torre; Arnold also leaves

In the winter of 1773–1774 the City Surveyor, searching for the City wells in Marylebone, discovered in the Gardens a spring alleged to be 'valuable'.

Thus Marybone, late in the day, joined the ranks of 'Spas', such as Bagnigge Wells, Sadlers Wells, Islington Wells, and others which boasted health-giving properties. The fashion for 'drinking the waters' had begun in the previous century, and would soon be superseded by the latest craze: sea bathing. Meanwhile, Marybone welcomed an additional attraction. The waters were said to 'strengthen the stomach' and promote a good appetite and digestion; they might even be useful for nervous and scorbutic disorders.

From 6 June 1774 the Gardens were open every morning at 6.0 for water drinking and breakfast. Evening concerts began on 21 May. The Barthelemons had left, and James Hook had gone to Vauxhall, where he was to remain for nearly half a century. The chief singers were Miss Wewitzer (well known as the sister of a singing actress of Covent Garden), Miss Trelawney, Miss Wilde, Mr. Dubellamy, Mr. Webb and Mr. Reinhold, with Dr. Arnold presumably in sole charge of the music.

Subscription tickets at two guineas for two people were obtainable at the Gardens and from Mr. Piguenit, but did not admit in bad weather or on Sundays. On Sundays the

Soverign of Cates, all hail! Nor thou refuse
This cordial Offering, from an english Muse.
Who pours the Brandy in Libation free,
And finds Plumb-Pudding realiz'd in thee!

Plate 10. Miss Trusler.

Plate 11. A song sung at Marybone Gardens.

Plate 12. A song sung at Marybone Gardens.

Plate 13. A song sung at Marybone Gardens.

Plate 14. A song sung at Marybone Gardens.

G.S. CAREY.

Perry & Co Sculp Paternoster Row.

Publish'd as the Act directs, April 26, 1776.

Plate 15. George Saville Carey.

Plate 16. Admission tokens to Marybone Gardens.

Plate 17. The Apotheosis of Thomas Lowe.

Gardens were open after 5.0 p.m., without any entertainment, for which privilege 6d was charged, returnable 'in kind': tea, coffee and 'Ranelagh rolls'.

Accounts have been preserved for the second half of June 1774, and it is interesting to see that on three (presumably) fine Sundays there was an average taking at the 'Town Gate' (i.e. via 'The Rose' in the High Street) of £10, and at the 'Field Gate' of £12, which means that about 1,000 people must have enjoyed the fresh air, tea, coffee and Ranelagh rolls on Sundays.

Messrs. Caillot and Clitherow were 'Fireworkers', but Signor Torre remained in a class apart, and advertised proudly that he exhibited 'by Virtue of a Licence from the Board of Ordnance'.

His 'Exhibitions' were certainly unique, and their popularity was reflected in the takings. For instance, early in the season he announced that 'at the Request of several Persons of Distinction' he would exhibit on 31 May:

THE FORGE OF VULCAN under MOUNT AETNA
The CAVERN of the CYCLOPS
And FLOWING OF THE LAVA

Which he will perform (for the first time in England) in the same splendid Manner in which it was exhibited before the Court of France last year, on the Marriage of his Royal Highness the Count of Artois.

Signore Torre, unused to fallacies, too common in advertisements, rests the credit of this and of his future Exhibitions on their own Merits only.

The additions to this Representation consist principally in a Battle between Mars and his attendant Warriors against Vulcan and his Cyclops; Vulcan, stimulated by Jealousy, exerts his utmost efforts, and after a furious contest overwhelms his Adversary in the Eruption of the Lava.

After the 'Exhibition' there would be a 'magnificent Firework', thus making it clear that there was a distinction between these 'exhibitions' and a firework display.

This programme, which included 'a Grand Concert of vocal and instrumental Music' (in smaller print), was repeated at least nine times. At the ninth performance, 28 June, the takings greatly exceeded anything recorded for music during that period, except for Dr. Arnold's Benefit.

This occasion, designated 'The COMPOSER'S NIGHT', on 30 June, brought over £140. The main offering was a new burletta by Arnold himself, with words by D. J. Piguenit (the Treasurer, bookseller now of Berkeley Square) entitled *Don Quixote*. In this, Miss Wewitzer, Miss Wilde, Mrs. Ward, Mr. Smith, Mr. Dubellamy and Mr. Reinhold sang. Mr. Fisher, a pupil of Mr. Pinto, played a concerto on the violin.

But the first half of this programme featured 'Signor Caillot and his Firework', the word 'Firework' being in slightly larger print than the title of the burletta itself. Caillot promised many and very beautiful Pieces; 'Sensible of the Indulgence with which the Public have ever treated his Attempts to merit their Favour rests his Claim to Public Patronage on the Merit of his Exhibitions'. But he did not attempt anything in the Torre line. In addition, the Gardens would be splendidly illuminated with many thousand lamps of different colours.

When *Don Quixote* was repeated on 18 August for the Benefit of the author, Mr. Piguenit, Messrs. Caillot *and* Clitherow provided fireworks:

> The Artists will fire alternately. An Emulation in which the Applause of the Company will stimulate them to show their utmost Abilities in this capital Display,

and after this display they would attempt for the first time a burlesque Exhibition entitled THE FORGE OF VULCAN, the 'Music adapted to the Entertainment'. On this occasion also Mr. Carey would speak an 'Imitative Poetical Address for this Night only, introducing a favourite Air in the Character of Mr. Jerry Sneak'. Was this burlesque of

Torre's 'Forge of Vulcan' good-humoured or spiteful? Much later – after Torre's death – 'Mount Aetna', with the cavern of Vulcan, etc., was shown at Ranelagh in May 1792, but how close this was to the original it is impossible to guess. Torre must have been difficult to imitate, and still more difficult to burlesque.

There were revivals of *The Regret*, *The Wedding Day*, *Il Dilettante* and *La Serva Padrona*. Something new was Arnold's *Ode to Music* (originally given for the installation of Lord North as Chancellor of Oxford), with Miss Wilde, Miss Wewitzer, Mr. Reinhold and Mr. Webb, and a number of the best chorus singers. Afterwards there would be Select Songs and familiar Pieces in the Orchestra, and a Concerto on the German Flute, by 'the celebrated Mons. Rudell, Musician to the King of Portugal'. Apparently there were no fireworks planned for the evening, and the takings were very poor at both Gates.

An innovation on 6 July was a series of 'lectures' called 'A School of Shakespeare' to be given in the Burletta Theatre by Dr. Kenrick, a hack writer 'not without merit' according to Boswell, who lectured on every conceivable topic at the Devil Tavern, Temple Bar, and had virulently attacked both Johnson and Boswell. Johnson described him as 'one of the many who have made themselves public without making themselves *known*'.

Dr. Kenrick was apparently suffering at the time under a sense of grievance not unusual in the second-rate; he had been 'insidiously deprived' of certain emoluments, and therefore the intended publication of his Text of Shakespeare would have to be deferred after twenty years' work. He proposed to print the text in Four Volumes Octavo, price One Guinea Bound, and to deliver the Observations in the form of lectures, transferred for the summer season from the Apolo (*sic*), Devil Tavern to the Theatre at Marybone Gardens.

The audience were at first somewhat at a loss to comprehend the nature of the entertainment to which they were invited, but the Doctor assured them that there was a good precedent for holding such a function in a Public Garden: Plato's Discourses were read aloud in the environs of Athens.

The 'Introductory Address' on 6 July was to be a lecture, 'Serious and Comic on the "First Part of King Henry IV"', 'in which the composition of the drama, with the character of the King, of the Prince of Wales, of Hotspur and Sir John Falstaff will be particularly illustrated'. This implies some sort of dramatic recitation on the part of Dr. Kenrick. There would be a concert, vocal and instrumental, at 6.30, and the lecture at 8.30 precisely. Between the 'Parts' of the lecture, settings of Shakespeare songs would be sung, including 'Where the Bee sucks', probably in the still well loved Arne setting.

On 18 July there was another innovation: a so-called Fête Champêtre. 'Many of the decorations used at the Oaks would adorn the Gardens.' Lord Stanley had been married to the Lady Betty Hamilton in June, and he gave a Fête at Epsom on the occasion, which cost £9,000 (according to rumour). Horace Walpole said that all the orange trees round London had been bought up, and perhaps these (second-hand) had been procured for Marybone.

The Managers were attacked in the press for charging five shillings for an entertainment which consisted in 'a few tawdry festoons and extra lights'. Some of the discontented visitors broke a few lights in protest.

'Managers' in the plural probably alluded to Dr. Arnold and Mr. John Berry. John Berry Esq. was apparently the business manager to whom the staff at Marybone were accountable for their expenditure. Probably Arnold ran the musical side. 1774 seems to have been Arnold's last season, and this may account for the disappearance of regular musical evenings.

The profits from fireworks must have been illegal in a sense, because fireworks were 'contrary to the Injunction'.

(There seems to have been nobody to enforce these Injunctions[10].)

1774 was Torre's last year, and it is perhaps appropriate to take our leave of him at his patron Garrick's Fête Champêtre in the lovely riverside gardens of Hampton on 27 August. 'A most brilliant Firework and the Forge of Vulcan' entertained Garrick's guests. Garrick himself seemed less than enthusiastic about 'Rockets, Squibs and Crackers', but perhaps he was tired after the party and also shocked at the bill[11].

Torre's name was soon to be associated with the publication of Bartolozzi's new coloured stippled prints, and other delicate productions, rather than with spectacular fireworks and life-sized performances of classical myths. This remarkably versatile man, who was able to envisage and carry out projects on such a grand scale, also worked in a field requiring the minutest accuracy. In 1778, only four years after he had given up his pyrotechnical activities, he supplied the Paris Observatoire with two of his thermometers. 'A genius in his way,' Garrick called him. We might call him a genius in many ways, or at least a man of remarkable abilities. He is also honoured as the founder of the world renowned firm of art dealers, Colnaghi's[12].

Torre was unique, but fireworks continued at Marybone.

What had happened to Mrs. Fountain and her fellow-protestors? Is it possible that they had become accustomed to the noise, and even to enjoy the spectacle? It is pleasant to think that Mrs. Fountain's Young Ladies, having retired to rest at nine o'clock, sometimes crept out of bed and watched the night sky illuminated by magical patterns of coloured fire.

VIII
1775

*End of regular concerts; Miscellaneous entertain-
ments; Baddeley and his Magic Lantern; George
Saville Carey lectures on mimicry; Fireworks continue without Torre*

In 1775 there were no regular concerts. This simple statement
rings the knell of Marybone as conceived by Daniel Gough
and his successors. No more orchestras 'of the best Hands',
no more singers, no more Handel, Boyce, Hook, Arne,
Arnold and the rest. It had been a struggle for many years
to balance the accounts. Samuel Arnold's departure was the
end of an epoch. London musical life was the poorer.

Possibly because they knew that Torre was leaving, the
Magistrates had granted Marybone a Licence for 1775.
Nothing was said about fireworks one way or the other; there
were merely the usual provisos of 'no disorder', 'not to open
on Christmas Day' or before five in the afternoon, etc. (see
Appendix). Perhaps they were prepared to turn a blind eye
(and a deaf ear) to any fireworks but Torre's.

Dr. Kenrick's series of Shakespeare lectures seems to have
come to an abrupt end, but John Berry, or whoever was
now in charge, produced a series of miscellaneous entertainments.

On 3 June Robert Baddeley, husband of Sophia who had
sung at the Gardens in 1770, introduced what was still a
comparative novelty, the Magic Lantern. The Magical or
Optical Lantern had been invented over a century before.
It was a small optical device enabling you to see in the dark

various images in translucent colours projected on to a screen. This seemed sufficiently wonderful, not to say frightening, as it was often used to depict monsters and spectres. In France showmen toured the fairs with images of religious subjects, the terrors of hell being especially popular. But in 1771 the Abbé Nollet had managed to produce movement in his figures (e.g. a woman curtseying) by an elementary device. This was a great marvel.

But at this stage in its development the achievements of the Magic Lantern were more scenic than dramatic. Baddeley described his entertainment as 'an Attempt at a sketch of the Times in a Variety of Caricatures accompanied with a whimsical and satirical Dissertation on each Character'.

An Exordium was spoken at eight o'clock. Part I consisted in: A Modern Widow; A Sergeant-at-Law; a Bilking Courtesan; Andrew Marvell; a Modern Patriot; a Duelling Apothecary; a Foreign Quack; and Part II: A Man of Consequence; a Hackney Parson; a Robin Hood Orator; Lady Tit-for-Tat; an Italian Toothdrawer; High Life in St. Giles's; a Jockey; a Jew Catechism; and Part III: a 'short magic Sketch' called 'Punch's election'. Admission was 2s. 6d. including tea or coffee.

Some of these characters certainly seemed to call for action, but Baddeley was a good enough actor to cover up any shortcomings with his 'whimsical and satirical Dissertation'.

Baddeley was already one of the most successful comedians of his generation, and in 1777 would be the first Moses in *The School for Scandal*. In his early life he had travelled Europe as a valet, and his quick ear and gift for mimicry enabled him to store in his memory accents and mannerisms upon which he drew during his stage career. He left a sum of money which has provided an annual Twelfth Night Cake to be cut and eaten on the stage of Drury Lane on 6 January ever since his death in 1794.

On 21, 23 and 25 June, George Saville Carey (who had

contributed to Mr. Piguenit's Benefit the previous year) gave what he called a Lecture, which we should call a One Man Show, consisting in imitations of famous actors: Garrick and Mrs. Hartley, for instance, also Miss Catley and Mr. Dubellamy, who were both Marybone performers. Shakespearean characters were introduced, and some retrospective fun poked at the Stratford Jubilee and the Shakespeare cult in general: 'The Mulberry Tree', 'Sweet Willy O', 'Ye Warwickshire Lads', and so on.

George Saville Carey (see plate 15) was the posthumous son of Henry Carey – poet, musician and writer of burlesques, associated in most people's minds with 'Sally in our Alley'. George was also a writer, but his greatest fame was as a lecturer and mimic, and it was in that capacity that he appeared at Marybone. He wrote an essay on mimicry considered authoritative.

His chief claim to be remembered, however, is through his daughter, politely described by some as 'an itinerant actress', who in 1789 became the mother of Edmund Kean.

Fireworks continued. On 21 June, for instance, Carey's 'Lecture on Mimicry' was followed by the Forge of Vulcan, the Flowing of the Lava and the Cavern of the Cyclops, in honour of His Majesty's birthday. The display was described 'By Authority of His Majesty's Board of Ordnance', and was part of a Torre 'programme', carried out not by the master himself but apparently by Monsieur Caillot.

Complaints from local residents gained one advantage – better parking facilities:

> The Nobility and Gentry who favour the Manager of this Place with their Company are most respectfully requested to direct their Servants to drive their Carriages into that Piece of Ground prepared and properly lighted-up for that Purpose. Staff-men are employed to direct the Coachmen and call their Carriages.

The Manager (note the singular, presumably Mr. Berry) clearly hoped for 'Carriage Company', with its prestige and money.

The Waiters' Benefit (always late in the season) had been rained off, but they were granted another Night, 21 September, with a variety of entertainments, including 'The Forge of Vulcan', etc., given by Monsieur Caillot, followed by a large hot air balloon, illuminated with blazing stars. Let us hope that the waiters had a good 'gate', and were not robbed of their reward on the way home.

Signor Rossi also worked as pyrotechnist in September advertising 'fireworks' rather than 'exhibitions'.

IX
1776

Charles Dibdin's Puppets; Philip Breslaw and his Birds; Mrs. Stuart's Festival; The Boulevards of Paris; Miscellaneous Concerts; Fireworks by a former assistant of Torre; THE END

1776 is associated in the minds of most of us today with the War of American Independence. The Fourth of July had little direct impact upon visitors to Gardens such as Marybone. But there was certainly an uneasiness in many people's minds. We did not seem to be winning this distant American War. There were those who saw some parallel between the situation of Great Britain and the Roman Empire, whose 'Decline and Fall' had appeared early in the year. Horace Walpole thought this country was 'undone'.

Most people, however, whatever their views about the American War or the Roman Empire, had heard of David Garrick, even if they had never seen him. When he said farewell to the stage on 10 June it was the end of an epoch. It took Sir Joshua Reynolds three days to recover from the emotions this occasion aroused. Duchesses and Countesses crowded into the Upper Boxes just to get a distant view of the hero.

But Garrick had his enemies, and one of these was Charles Dibdin, who had worked for him as a kind of House Composer at Drury Lane, a situation which led to friction, since Garrick regarded music as at best 'pickle to his roast beef'. Dibdin's final grievance was that Garrick had taken his piece called *May Day or the Little Gipsy* and adapted it for himself with music by Dr. Arne, putting it on the stage in October 1775.

Dibdin planned a revenge; he further adapted *May Day* and called it *May Day or the Little Chimney Sweep*, and meant to have it performed by chimney sweeps on the Adelphi Terrace outside Garrick's home. For some reason he changed the original plan, and instead brought out a puppet entertainment called *The Comic Mirror* at the elegant little Theatre in Exeter Change. The Puppets (or Fantoccini) represented various subjects for gossip, such as the Ranelagh Regatta of 1775, the trial for bigamy of the Duchess of Kingston, and Garrick himself. There is no previous record of Dibdin as a puppet-maker or manipulator. He probably had the Garrick figure especially made for him, as a good likeness would have been essential.

In the summer of 1776 when Garrick fever was at its height Dibdin took his show to Marybone, advertising it as The World in Miniature. Part I consisted of *An Exact Representation of the Orchestra at Work* with 'several favourite Songs'; Part II was a serenata called *The Milkmaid*, followed by *The Spouting Club*, including 'many new imitations', in which the Garrick puppet probably appeared, and *The Recruiting Sergeant*; Part III was *Shylock's Plot*, probably an impersonation of Macklin's Shylock, known to have been a part of the entertainment. A Grand Finale which included a naval review was entitled WELCOME HOME.

Dibdin's own verdict on the entertainment was that 'it contained nothing malignant' and 'ran its day'.

He went to France at the end of the season, leaving his puppets behind. They were stored in the Temple of Apollo, according to his own account, and when this was demolished the Duchess of Kingston, David Garrick and the rest were buried in the ruins[13]. This is a pretty story, but Dibdin was not in England at the time of the Gardens' closure, and it will be seen that in 1777 the puppets were put up for auction (see p. 124).

There must have been singers as well as speakers behind the scenes in this entertainment, and enough instruments to represent an orchestra. But no names are given and the show was in no sense a concert.

Everything was done by Berry (and possibly a colleague called Henslow) to attract a public apparently tired of the old formula of music, fireworks and refreshment in rural surroundings, without spending too much money. After 'Lectures', a Magic Lantern and Puppets had been tried, a conjuror was introduced.

Philip Breslaw, a Jew of German origin who specialised in juggling, card tricks, sleight of hand of various kinds, thought-reading and performing birds, first appeared in England in the early 1770s or even earlier and was at the Exhibition Room in Cockspur Street in 1772. This was fitted up with pit and boxes, and illuminated by candles. Breslaw had musical assistants: Signore Nicola and Madame Romaldo, singers, and Signor Romain who played the violin 'in many different attitudes'. There was also Signor Rossignol, a bird imitator, and a company of birds, drilled apparently by Breslaw himself, who marched and countermarched like soldiers. The performing birds seem to have been the most original part of Mr. Breslaw's programme, but his thought-reading was considered remarkable:

> Mr. Breslaw will exhibit many new and astonishing deceptions on Cards, Letters, Thoughts, Numbers, etc., and particularly he will tell the Ladies their real Thoughts without asking any questions.

On Wednesday, 3 June, Mr. Breslaw brought his musicians, his 'deceptions' and presumably also his birds to Marybone, and announced his intention of performing there on Mondays, Wednesdays and Fridays, continuing at the Cockspur Room on Tuesdays, Thursdays and Saturdays[14].

On 25 June a Festivale di Campagna was held 'under the Direction of Mrs. Stuart', who rented the Gardens for the

evening. A new Temple of Apollo was erected, probably
made of canvas, lath and plaster, described as a very elegant
Fabric of the Doric Order, adorned with pillars, pilasters
and transparent paintings, superior to the Colonnade at
Ranelagh, both in proportions and illumination. The trans-
parencies were the work of 'the ingenious Signor Rebecca'[15].
Mrs. Stuart had herself paid for the erection of this new
Temple of Apollo, 'intended as a ballroom'.

Tickets for two persons were one guinea and a half, and
one guinea for one person, obtainable from Mrs. Stuart herself at 40 Portland Street, from the indispensable Mr. Piguenit in Berkeley Square, from Mr. White, the Hatter, in
Panton Street, or at the Gardens. But there would be no
admission without tickets, and no paying at the door.

The entertainment was to begin at 8.30 with a concert
of vocal and instrumental music lasting till ten o'clock, after
which there would be catches and glees in different parts
of the Gardens. A cold Collation would be served at eleven
o'clock, and dancing to a band would commence at midnight.
In one part of the Gardens there would be a representation
of the Alameida of Cadiz, where orgeat and lemonade would
be served. Dancers were engaged to perform in fancy dress;
in particular two sets of fairies would appear. Mrs. Stuart
promised: 'The greatest Attention will be made to render
the Evening's Entertainment elegant and complete.'

It all sounds like the best days of Marybone, music and
all. But the reality does not seem to have fulfilled Mrs.
Stuart's promises. The *Public Advertiser* certainly praised
her Temple of Apollo, and the illuminations, particularly
'the spiral Chandeliers', but some decorations consisted merely of paper ribbons twisted round trees, and festoons of
stuff hanging from the boxes. The Alameida of Cadiz seems
to have been detained by contrary winds, and the orgeat
and lemonade were conspicuous by their absence. The two
sets of fairies were as invisible as the Alameida. Catches
and Glees, however, were performed (perhaps a repeat of the

Dr. Arne performances of 1773–1774?). There were only about a dozen masks and fancy dresses but, according to the Correspondent who reported the entertainment in the press, there were various Lords and Ladies, and their Foreign Ministers. One has a suspicion that he wrote tongue in cheek.

1776 saw a revival of masquerades and masks, which caused the year to be known as the Year of Masquerades. After having been banned for several years they returned in a slightly different form, organised by Clubs which issued a limited number of tickets. There were such entertainments at Vauxhall and Ranelagh in the summer and at Mrs. Cornelys' establishment in Soho Square, known as Carlisle House. Mrs. Stuart may have been hoping to be another Mrs. Cornelys.

The Festivale di Campagna did not quite come up to her expectations, nor to those of anybody else. She wrote to the *Morning Post* complaining that the Proprietors of Marybone had dealt very ungenerously with her. She was sole proprietor of 'the elegant Room' erected in the Gardens, but she had not been given the least part of the profits it had brought to a place 'deserted by the public'.

But her efforts had not been in vain. On 27 June, two days after the first showing of the Festivale, there was a new Grand Exhibition of Mr. Breslaw and his New Italian Company, which would give the Public an Opportunity to view the Alameida of Cadiz and the magnificent Ballroom, built on purpose for the Festivale. Presumably the Alameida, which the *Public Advertiser* sneeringly thought to have been detained by contrary winds, had now arrived at Marybone in all its splendour.

There were to be further repetitions of the Festivale, although one or two of these seem to have been cancelled because of unfavourable weather. On 4 July the *World in Miniature* was revived as an additional entertainment and included a representation of the Ranelagh Regatta, Canal, Gardens, Colonnade, etc., and well known characters performed. A 'Capital Firework' was to end the evening.

On Thursday, 11 July, Mrs. Stuart was given a Benefit. The Ballroom, which even in its imperfect state had given 'universal Satisfaction', was now completed, and various additions would be made to the Gardens, including transparent Fruit Trees, and the Alameida would be 'perfected'. The printer seems to have been so overcome at this prospect that in large letters he promised the public the LALA MADE DE CADIZ.

The doors would not be open until eight o'clock because of the brilliance of the illuminations. There would be a repeat of *The World in Miniature*, and an elegant Firework to finish the evening.

There was a last flicker of rococo gaiety in another Al Fresco Entertainment, the Boulevards of Paris, given on 25 July. It was a scene 'equally novel and agreeable'. The boxes facing the ballroom were converted into shops with signs indicating what they sold: Newfangle was a milliner, and so was Blonde; Tête was a hairdresser exhibiting tall headdresses, probably not so tall as those of some of his potential customers, however, for 1776 saw high head-dressing at its most extreme. The salesmen and saleswomen were appropriately dressed. Crotchet sold music, and Medley was a print shop. The ballroom, illuminated with coloured lamps, represented the English coffee house at Paris, selling not coffee, it seems, but 'cooling Drinks'.

In an outdoor booth belonging to Signor Nicola eight 'Gentlemen exhibited War Dances and climbed on one another's Shoulders to represent the Egyptian Pyramids'. In the Saloon there was 'a curious Exhibition' of the Ruins of Rome. There were country sports out of doors, there were Italian Performers to entertain with 'comic Music' (*sic*), Fantoccini to perform *The Comic Mirror*, a show of stuffed birds, and finally 'an elegant Firework'.

The number of persons present was estimated at 600. The affair seems to have been quite decorous, except for the appearance of 'three masculine Figures in the Dresses of Arcadian Shepherdesses' who were certainly the worse for drink.

On the fourth evening of the Boulevards of Paris the Illuminated Temple, described as giving 'Universal Satisfaction', was the setting for a pyrotechnical display 'never performed in England', 'un Combat entre trois Dragons'. This may have been a speciality of Monsieur Caillot, but dragons were popular with pyrotechnists. Ron Harris says that green dragons and monsters in general used to be covered with Muscovy Glass, which allowed fire to shine through, and if deep-coloured would glow in a suitable ghost-like manner.

On 11 and 17 June, in honour of the King's birthday, Monsieur Caillot produced 'a new Piece' entitled *La Cavalea d'Arlequino e di Piero*, presumably on some Commedia dell'Arte theme.

The setting of the Boulevards of Paris seems to have been retained until the end of the season, occasionally with 'Alterations and Additions'.

These included tumbling, vaulting, the slack rope and other 'Country Sports'; there were exhibitions of the Ruins of Rome and also of stuffed exotic birds; the *Mirror* would begin with *The Recruiting Sergeant*; then Mr. Carey would give the first part of his Lecture on Mimicry in 'the beautiful Room'; then there was to be more *Comic Mirror*, after which Mr. Breslaw would give his 'much admired Deceptions' in 'the *Great* Room'.

Presumably the puppets performed the *Mirror* in the Burletta Theatre, so that the audience had to move from one venue to another if they were to get their money's worth. Out of doors Monsieur Caillot promised an Exhibition Extraordinary in Fourteen Divisions.

Musicians engaged for the 1776 season or part of it included Mr. Hutton, Mr. Howell, Mr. Dighton, Mr. Thackray and Miss Thomas. On the occasion of Mr. Hutton's Benefit, Mr. Palmer and Mr. Simpson played concertos on the German flute and the violin respectively. A Miss Abrahams also played on the violin. Probably there was an orchestra.

The most interesting name is that of Dighton, later well known as singer, actor and caricaturist. According to the *Biographical Dictionary*[16], his name was first billed as a performer at the Haymarket in 1777, a year after this Marybone appearance. But the *Biographical Dictionary* rightly surmises that he had probably been singing at London Pleasure Gardens before that date.

On the last few nights of 1776 Sieur Mastaeus, who described himself as having been for eleven years a pupil and for several years an assistant of Signor Torre, advertised a varied programme of fireworks. One particularly elaborate programme was described as 'in the Stile of Signor Torre', but it seemed to have no dramatic content which could be compared with the Torre 'Exhibitions'.

The Gardens finally closed on 23 September, after several postponements. The evening was for the Benefit of the waiters, and was a typical 1776 variety of Entertainments, including an 'Address to the Town' by a Master Russel, and ending with a Most Magnificent Firework, which filled the sky with colour and patterns in a last gesture of defiance to the Magistrates and all protesters.

It seems unlikely that the Gardens were ever re-opened.

In the summer of 1777 the 'Sunday Rambler' visited what was left of the Gardens with apparently no admission formalities at the Gate. He wrote that the Gardens consisted of 'no more than two or three gravel roads' (*sic*), and a few shapeless trees. The places intended for company displayed tables made of unplaned wood wretchedly put together and still covered with dirty tablecloths. Those parts which might have resembled a garden were clogged with rubbish and lumber, remaining from Signor Torre and 'other ingenious imitators of the infernal regions'. An old gentleman told the writer that the Music Licence had nearly expired, and the proprietors did not think it worth while to put the Gardens

into repair until they knew whether it would be renewed
or not.

On Wednesday, 2 April 1777, there appeared in Number
14443 of the *Public Advertiser* the following:

> To be Sold by Auction by C. D. PIGUENIT
> On the Premises, Tomorrow, and the two following Days
>   at Eleven.
> The Materials of many substantial Buildings, the Boxes,
> Tables, and Benches, now standing in Marybone Gardens.
> At the same time will be sold the remarkable fine toned and
> seasoned Organ, many Lots of useful Household Furniture,
> Table Linen, China and c . . . (illegible) several elegant Glass
> Chandeliers; the Stock of excellent Wines, and several
> Hundred Globe and other Lamps, &c. On the last day will
> be sold, in one Lot, the Scenes, Musick, Lamps and about
> 40 Puppets, belonging to the favourite Entertainment the
> Comick Mirror, and an Excellent Harpsichord, by the late
> Mr. Joseph Merlin, a Collection of Printed and Manuscript
> Musick &c. To be viewed. Catalogues may be had . . . (at)
> the Virginia Coffee House; and of C. D. Piguenit, Berkeley
> Square.

A diligent search of newspapers subsequent to the date
of the sale has yielded no account of either its financial result
or of the purchasers. An exception is a would-be humorous
account of the affair, lampooning various well-known characters.

Among the cuttings in a scrap book at the Royal College
of Music there is a paragraph headed 'Intelligence from Marybone Gardens', and in the Crace Collection at the Westminster (Marylebone) Library there are some abbreviated
manuscript notes from this same paragraph, as if taken in
a hurry, with a date in April 1777, which might be 10 or
18 (more likely the latter) and 'MP' beside it.

Here are a few examples of 'capital bidders' to whom various 'articles' were alleged to have been knocked down:

Mount Aetna, with all the combustibles of Gunpowder,
Fire and Brimstone to the Marchioness of Q——
as a Cushion to her Tête.

(Probably the Duchess of Queensberry, the beautiful though
somewhat eccentric 'Kitty', celebrated by Swift, Gay and
Walpole, who kept her beauty until well on into her seventies,
and died in July 1777 from eating too many cherries. A Tête
was the fashionable high head-dress which needed a cushion
to support it.)

The Bar, to Mrs. Caroline Rudd, for it is well
known that no woman has cut so great a figure at
the Bar.

(Mrs. Rudd had recently been acquitted of a charge of forgery, in a *cause célèbre*.)

All the empty Boxes and Seats to Mr. L——y of the
Theatre Royal, Drury Lane.

(Mr. Lacy was at one time joint manager.)

And so on. The attributions may have been more entertaining to scandal-mongers of the period than they are to us.

We should like to know the real fate of Dibdin's puppets,
alleged to have been purchased by G——e C——l——an
Esq. to be brought out 'this summer' at the Theatre Royal
in the Haymarket, the puppet which resembled Dr. A——e
being smuggled out and given to his favourite lady. G——e
C——l——n was George Colman, and Dr. A——e of course
Dr. Arne, but we neither know nor care who was his favourite
lady in the year 1777.

It is possible, George Speaight suggests, that the puppets
were bought by Flockton, a noted puppet master of the
time who was performing between 1762 and 1788, and
whose repertory included at least one of Dibdin's comic
operas.

The last Licence for 'The Rose' was issued in 1775, but might well have been carried over until 1776. A Music Licence had been issued to Samuel Arnold and John Berry in 1774 for 1775; the fact that none can be found for 1776 does not prove anything either way since relatively few of these Licences have survived (see Appendix).

The Rate Books provide the most reliable evidence. In 1778 no rates were paid for 'The Rose'; Nos. 35–38 Marylebone High Street are described as 'vacant' and No. 39 as 'in building'.

Thus 1778 saw the end of the Gardens as we know them. But it is not impossible that before all the buildings were demolished and the site was 'developed' there were some attempts at revival. In the British Museum there is a Marybone Token dated 1778 (compare Plate 16). Was this produced in advance in the hopes of a revival? If such a revival ever materialised, it could not have lasted long.

It is suggested by Gordon Mackenzie and others that, although the Gardens closed down in 1778, there was an attempt to revive them on some piece of ground left vacant in 1794. It is difficult to accept this theory, since Horwood's plan of 1792 shows the whole area laid out much as it is today.

But clearly both demolition of the solid buildings involved and building of the new streets which replaced them took ten years or more. Beaumont Street was inhabited by 1781, Beaumont Mews by 1790, Upper Wimpole Street by 1785. The old Manor House was pulled down in 1791.

The new streets were spaciously laid out, and the many houses which have survived are worthy examples of the good proportions and dignity of the late eighteenth century. Most of them still serve the medical profession with which this part of London has become associated. The High Street is a lively shopping centre, with a high proportion of boutiques, luxury food shops and restaurants. The BBC Publications stand where the main entrance to the Gardens used to be, and a garage occupies the site of Dr. Fountain's school.

Nothing remains to remind us of the mid-eighteenth-century rococo of Marybone Gardens.

Nor is there any equivalent of the kind of entertainment once offered by the Gardens.

North of the 'New Road' the 412 acres of Regents Park certainly provide what Mr. Trusler would have called 'a pleasant Airing', but on a scale and catering for a number of people he could never have envisaged in his plans for Marybone Gardens.

Not only the acreage but also the amenities provided would have surprised the Nobility and Gentry who frequented London Pleasure Gardens. As the nineteenth century progressed people developed a taste for more active pursuits than strolling along tree-lined avenues. Physical exercise as well as fresh air was considered necessary to health. There had to be provision for ball games, some of them hitherto unknown except on the village green. Regents Park could also provide aquatic sports in the form of boating on the Lake.

Flowers, which were never of prime importance in the eighteenth-century Pleasure Gardens, became essential features of nineteenth- and twentieth-century places of public recreation.

Fauna were as little on public view as flora in the eighteenth century. If you wanted to see wild animals you had to go to the Menagerie at the Tower of London. Since 1828 there has been a Zoological Garden in Regents Park.

Three features, however, reminds us of Marybone: tea, coffee and all kinds of 'Liquor and Provisions' may be obtained out of doors; there is an 'Orchestra' in the Park, called a Bandstand nowadays; and there is an Outdoor Theatre. Performances take place under cover if wet, a reminder that whatever else may have changed the English climate remains the chief enemy of all al fresco entertainment.

Notes to Part Four

1 W. T. Parke: *Musical Memoirs*, 1830.
2 Roger Fiske: *English Theatre Music in the Eighteenth Century*, OUP, 1973.
3 Invaluable information has been given on eighteenth-century fireworks, particularly on Torre's 'Exhibitions', by Mr. Ron Harris. Without his help it would have been impossible to visualise these entertainments.
4 Donald Garstang: *Colnaghi: Art, Commerce, Scholarship, 1760–1984*, London, 1984.
5 *The Letters of David Garrick*, edited by David M. Little and George M. Kahrl, London, OUP, 1963.
6 See Appendix on Licences.
7 *The Letters of David Garrick, supra.*
8 James Boswell: *Life of Johnson*, Vol. III, p. 382 (Macmillan ed., 1912).
9 Catalogue to Kenwood Exhibition, 1985: *Joseph Merlin, the Ingenious Mechanick.*
10 Appendix on Licences, *supra.*
11 *The Letters of David Garrick, supra.*
12 Donald Garstang, *supra*; and further information supplied by him.
13 Charles Dibdin the Elder: *Professional Life*, 1803.
14 Information kindly supplied by Professor E. A. Dawes, PhD, DSc, FRIC.
15 Biagio Rebecca's work can still be seen in various English country houses. See Sacheverell Sitwell: *British Architects and Craftsmen*, 2nd edition, 1946–1947.
16 Philip H. Highfill Jr., Kalman A. Burnim, Edward Langhans: *A Biographical Dictionary of Actors, Actresses, Musicians, Dancers, Managers and other Stage Personnel in London, 1666–1806*, Southern Illinois University Press, USA, 1973.

Appendix

Licences preserved in the Archives of the (former) GLC Record Office

Such applications for Licences as have been preserved in the (former) GLC Record Office are here reproduced.

Sometimes a newspaper paragraph will state briefly whether an application has been granted or refused. Such mentions are in the text.

There seems to have been little attempt at enforcing a rejection, judging by the history of the years 1772–1774.

MJ/SP 1768 Oct./40

Application by Thomas Lowe Proprietor for licence for Marybone Gardens dated 6 October 1768 to the Justices of the Peace for the county of Middlesex at the Michaelmas Quarter Sessions.

The humble petition of Thomas Lowe sheweth that your petitioner was favoured with your worships' licence the last year for continuing the Publick Entertainment at Marybone Gardens which has been used for several years past in the Summer season for Publick musick and licensed by your worships according to the direction of the Act of Parliament for regulating Places of Entertainment. That while your petitioner shall be so happy as to be favoured by your worships with the continuance of that licence he shall study to preserve good order decorum therein in strict conformity to the said Act and your worships' direction in that behalf ...

Granted 20 October 1768

Appendix

5 October 1769 Michaelmas Quarter Sessions

Thomas Pinto and Samuel Arnold have purchased House and Gardens called Marybone Gardens since the last time of licensing . . . (thereafter similar wording to above).

Read and the Cons. adjc. till this day fortnight Hicks Hall

MJ/SP 1772 October 98

To Sir John Hawkins and Justices of the Peace at the Quarter Sessions of the Peace for Middlesex.

The Humble petition of Messrs. Arnold and Berry for many years proprietors of Marybone Gardens . . .

Conduct in management of gardens in past uncensured – no impediment to licence until last Michaelmas session which was occasioned by Signor Torree's exhibiting fireworks at their gardens. They were not instigators of Signor Torree's coming into the Kingdom, his design being to exhibit fireworks at Ranelagh Gardens but proprietors did not agree to his terms – they were persuaded by many respectable persons who assured them that if said Signor Torree could obtain licence from the Master of the Ordnance such exhibition not contrary to law. Signor Torree obtained licence – your petitioners considered exhibition of fireworks had been made in publick gardens upwards of 20 years without legality being questioned – had no idea of censure. Entered into contract with Signor Torree for whole term of lease of gardens, assigned part for that purpose; Signor Torree to erect buildings and they entered into a bond of £1,000 for observation of said contract. At last general licensing upon Dr. Arnold's application for licence he not expecting any objection would be made came unprepared with authority from Signor Torree or Mr. Berry to answer objections or to enter into any promise that might include them; such engagement would have subjected him to the penalty of his bond from Signor Torree and rendered him answerable to his partner. Could not be released from bond without judgement in law; if he had promised to discontinue fireworks upon his own authority would have been guilty of breach of his promise and incurred penalty of the bond. They would have prevailed upon Signor Torree to give up engagement and would have stopped exhibition of fireworks being unhappy at falling under Justices of the Peace censure. Unable to obtain release until last September. Gardens now in full possession of petitioners; if they now exhibit fireworks or suffer anything to be exhibited contrary to law good morals and decency censure should fall on their own heads. Ready to enter bond of recognisance in any sum court shall deem proper for confirmation of promise.

Plea for restoration of licence on above facts.

Rejected.

MR/LMD 1/11

Note . . . It is ordered that no licence be granted to the Proprietors of Ranelagh or Marybone Gardens or of any other place of Publick Entertainment, but under a restriction prohibiting the exhibition fireworks by the Court.

MR/LMD 1/24

Michaelmas Quarter Session for Middlesex 20 October 1774.

Licence granted to Samuel Arnold and John Berry for Marybone Gardens . . . provided no disorder takes place . . . not to open on Christmas Day, etc. . . . not to open before 5 in the afternoon . . .

Select Bibliography

The place of publication is London unless otherwise stated.

Angelo, Henry: *Reminiscences*, 1828–1830.

Barton, Nicholas: *The Lost Rivers of London*, 1963; republished 1982.

Bracco, Patrick, and Lubovici, Elizabeth: Introduction and Catalogue to *Fireworks, French Fireworks from the 17th to 19th century*, National Gallery of Art, Washington, D.C., 1976.

Brock, Alan St. H., A.R.I.B.A.: *A History of Fireworks*, 1949.

Bryan, C.P.: *Round about Harley Street*, 1972.

Burnim, Kalmar A.: see Highfill.

Carse, Adam: *The XVIII Century Orchestra*, Cambridge, 1940.

Clinch, George: *Marylebone and St. Pancras*, 1890.

Cox-Johnson: see Saunders.

Daniel, George: Typed notes on Marybone Gardens in Archives Department, Westminster City Libraries (Marylebone Library).

Davies, B. R.: *Topographical Survey of the Village of St. Marylebone*, 1834.

Dibdin, Charles the Elder: *Professional Life*, 1803.

Dictionary of National Biography.

Doran, Dr. John: *A Lady of the Last Century*, 1873.

Enciclopedia dello Spettacolo, Rome, 1954 *et seq.*

Fiske, Roger: *English Theatre Music in the Eighteenth Century*, OUP, 1973.

Foot, Edward: Typed and photocopied notes, Archives Department, Westminster City Libraries (Marylebone Library).

Gardiner, Florence: Corrected proofs of unpublished article, 1875; Archives Department, Westminster City Libraries (Marylebone Library).

Garrick, David: *The Letters of,* edited by David M. Little and George M. Kahrl, OUP, London, 1963.

133

Select Bibliography

Grove's Dictionary of Music and Musicians, 5th edition and 6th edition.

Highfill, Philip H. Jr., Burnim, Kalmar A., Langhans, Edward: *A Biographical Dictionary of Actors, Actresses, Musicians, Dancers, Managers and Other Stage Personnel in London, 1666–1806*, Southern Illinois University Press, USA, 1973.

Hone, William: *Yearbook*, 1838.

Jacobs, L.: *Streets of St. Marylebone*, 1955.

Langhans, Edward: See Highfill.

Lewis, W. S.: *Three Tours through London in the Years 1748, 1776, 1797*, New Haven, Yale University Press, 1941.

Mackenzie, Gordon: *Marylebone North of Oxford Street*, 1972.

Manchée, W. H.: *Proceedings of the Huguenot Society of London*, Vol. XI, No. 1, 1914–1915.

Quennell, Peter: *Alexander Pope*, 1968.

Rubens, Alfred: *Jews on the English Stage*, Transaction of the Jewish Historical Society of England, Vol. 24d, Misc., p. 168.

Saunders, Dr. Ann: *Regents Park*, 2nd edition revised, Bedford College, London, 1981.

Abroad in Marylebone, BBC Publications, 1941.

Sheppard, F. H. W.: *Local Government in St. Marylebone, 1688–1835*, University of London, 1958.

Smith, J. T.: *Nollekens and his Times*, 1828.

A Book for a Rainy Day, 1845; Wilfred Whitten edition, 1903.

Smith, Thomas: *A Topographical and Historical Account of the Parish of St. Marylebone*, 1833.

Speaight, George.: *The History of the English Puppet Theatre*, 1955.

Summerson, John: *Georgian London*, 1945.

Wroth, Warwick: *The London Pleasure Gardens of the Eighteenth Century*, 1896.

Index

abbreviations: b. (born); m. (married); n. (note); p., pp. (page, pages); *p., pls* (*plate, plates*); sr, jr (senior, junior)

Index

Index

'Ode in Honour of Shakespeare' (Arnold) 79
'Ode on Masonry' 65
'Ode to Music' (Arnold) 109
Orpheus and Euridice 100, 103

Padraio, Signor, firemaster 96
Palma, Signor, composer 31
Palmer, flautist 122–3
Parke, John, oboist 77
patrons 11, 14, 15–16, 30–1, 40–1, 44, 47, 50, 51, 64, 68, 71, 94, 102, 109–10; wooed by management 63, 77, 98, 108
    parking facilities 114
    safe-conduct guards 4, 26, 31, 58, 61, 69; wages 70
    see also admission charges
Pepys, Samuel 2
Phillips, singer 69, 96, 100, 102
Phillips, Master, singer 28
Philpot, organist 26, 28, 30
Piguenit, C. D. 124
Piguenit, D. J., treasurer 78, 84, 91, 106, 119; as librettist 108
Pinto, Mrs T. (b. Charlotte Brent) 75, 76, 79
Pinto, Thomas 75, 78, 79, 130
Plenius, Miss, singer 59, 61
'Polly of the Plain' 32
Prince of Wales, Frederick 5, 14–15
puppets, Dibdin's: *The Comic Mirror* or *The World in Miniature* 117–18, 120, 121, 122; sale 124; later possible buyer 125

Ramelio, Mrs, singer 31, 32
Ranelagh 2, 6, 16, 33–4, 40, 60, 88
Rathyen, horn player 67
Raworth, singer 63, 67
Rebecca, Biagio 119, 128n.15
Reeves, violinist 84

refreshments 11, 25, 26, 40–1, 48–9, 50, 63, 64, 68, 107, 113, 119, 121; major attraction 35–6, 47; catering equipment 36
    public breakfasts 15, 27, 28, 35, 40, 50, 106
    drinking the waters 106
Regrets, The, burletta 109
Reinhold, F. C., bass and organist 40, 81, 82, 84, 85, 96, 99, 100, 102, 106, 108, 109
'Return, O God of Hosts' (Handel) 32
Revenge, The (Arnold/Chatterton) 81
Reynolds (Reynoldson), singer 75, 76
Richards 78, 82
Rocque map 12; *pl.4*
Roderigo (Rodrigo), violinist 59, 61
Rogers of Bath, French horn 82
Rose, Henry, violinist 26
Rose of Normandy, 12, 21n.1, 58
Rose tavern 2, 4, 12, 14, 21n.1, 33, 44–5, 57, 58, 75, 107, 126
Rossi, firemaster 78, 84, 85, 115
Rossignol, Signor, bird mimic 118
Rudell, *Mons.*, flautist 109
Russel, Master 123
Russell, clergyman, protester 91

St Paul's choirboys 96
Sainthill map 2, 12; *figure* p. 3
Samson (Handel) 28, 30
Saratina, Signorina, singer 40
Scherzi delle Muse, Gli, musical 78
Scott, Misses, singers 17
Seipts, horn player 67
Serva Padrona, La, burletta as *The Servant Mistress* 37, 39, 40, 81–2, 84, 85, 96, 109

139